1987

CHAUCER STUDIES III

Essays on Troilus and Criseyde

CHAUCER STUDIES

I

MUSIC IN THE AGE OF CHAUCER
Nigel Wilkins

II

CHAUCER'S LANGUAGE AND THE PHILOSOPHERS' TRADITION
J. D. Burnley

Essays on
Troilus and Criseyde

Edited by Mary Salu

D. S. BREWER · ROWMAN & LITTLEFIELD

© Contributors 1979

First published by D. S. Brewer,
240 Hills Road, Cambridge
an imprint of Boydell & Brewer Ltd,
PO Box 9, Woodbridge, Suffolk IP12 3DF
and by Rowman and Littlefield, 81 Adams Drive,
Totowa, New Jersey N.J. 07512, USA

Reprinted 1982

British Library Cataloguing in Publication Data

Essays on 'Troilus and Criseyde'. – (Chaucer studies; 3).
1. Chaucer, Geoffrey. Troilus and Criseyde
I. Salu, Mary   II. Series
821'.1   PR1896

ISBN (UK) 0 85991 053 9
(US) 0 8476 6236 5

Printed in Great Britain by
Nene Litho Ltd
and bound by Woolnough Bookbinding
Wellingborough, Northants

Contents

Preface

The initiation of this volume was due to my former colleague, Mr John P. White of St Mary's College, Newcastle upon Tyne, who thought it worth while to gather together some contemporary essays on Chaucer's *Troilus and Criseyde*.

Interest in Chaucer's greatest serious poems has never been more eager. The range of approach in this book is wide, from a study of the textual matters, an attempt to find the aim of the poem, the standing of Chaucer in the learning and interests of his time, the details of technique, to a certain specific emphasis on Criseyde.

It is perhaps appropriate here to mention that Miss Woolf, who was writing for the volume at the time of her death, would have lent weight to the concentration with her essay, 'How many children had Criseyde?'

MARY SALU

Acknowledgements

I owe great debts to those who have aided me in the collecting and production of these essays.

My thanks go to Mr John P. White for its beginning, and very greatly to Mr John McKinnell for his most scholarly help in the editing.

In Memory of
Rosemary Estelle Woolf

The Text of the *Troilus*

BARRY WINDEATT

Chaucer's *Troilus and Criseyde* is by far his most ambitious single poem, and the MSS of this poem offer the most intricate and mysterious textual problems among the MSS of his works. Is there some connection here which stems from the hand of the poet himself? None of the surviving copies of the *Troilus* predate the early fifteenth century, yet is it possible to see some link between the ambitiousness and scope of the poet's aspirations and the intractable singularities of the extant MSS? The evidence of the *Troilus* MSS has been little examined, yet the intriguing nature of these MSS – by enabling us to understand how the poem came to exist in its present form and how it was first read – can contribute to our critical understanding of the poem as a whole.

To adapt Dr Johnson's advice on Shakespeare and read through the *Troilus* without its modern notes produces a very different impression of the poem from that gained when it is read with an eye on the annotations of its editors. The latter offer a kind of X-ray vision which takes us behind the very processes of the poem's composition and which soon reveals with what a patchwork and embroidery of inserted and expanded passages of varying sizes Chaucer has overlaid the existing structure of his main narrative source, Boccaccio's *Filostrato*. The range of his proven borrowings and innovations over any given passage of the poem indicates that Chaucer's composition of the *Troilus* was a process which involved distinctly different kinds of poetic activity, and that process may well

1

have affected the way the poet's own earliest draft developed as a material entity.

Chaucer might first set about simply rendering into English the narrative line that *Filostrato* offered him. Whether or not he also needed the dull French prose of Beauvau to help him grasp Boccaccio, Chaucer worked directly from the stanzaic Italian text, which determines his disposition of the material into his own stanzas and lines. Some of Chaucer's narrative expansions and modifications of *Filostrato* would no doubt occur to him now and could be worked in at this stage. But it would not be unlikely that further expansions – especially those rendering Chaucer's reading from a range of sources – would be added as the poet worked over his material subsequent to his first efforts at translating. Such expansions could be written directly on to his first working copy or perhaps inserted into his existing draft in some separate form.

But in whatever form his draft exactly developed, the range of his proven sources suggests that Chaucer's composition of the poem was in practice a series of layers – perhaps physical layers – of writing. It is a diverse creative process of translating, modifying, and versifying into English the *Filostrato* stanzas and of introducing other passages of borrowed and invented materials which need to be versified into the same stanza pattern. This is that important activity of *in-eching* into his source which Chaucer alludes to as part of the creative translating process behind the poem's present form ('And if that ich . . . Have any word in eched. for the beste . . .' III, 1328–30). During this composition process Chaucer transforms *Filostrato* by his cumulative addition of many reflective, philosophical passages which contribute to his distinctive account of Troilus and Criseyde.

Certain distinctions between some of the extant *Troilus* MSS have been widely accepted as evidence that Chaucer issued two or even three 'versions' of the poem during his lifetime, and the most substantial and striking of such differences concern the presence or absence in the MSS of some of these philosophical passages. But it is symptomatic of the textual problem presented by the *Troilus* MSS that the principal editors and critics concerned with the problem have produced different interpretations of the same material. For Root[1] the MSS revealed the existence (in a minority of MSS) of a first, earlier version of the poem (Root's 'α'), distinguished by some omissions and a number of detailed readings. To Root the remaining majority of the MSS represented the 'revised version' of the poem. But within this body of MSS he distinguished two states of the poem after 'α', which he thought were descended from Chaucer's poem at different stages of the poet's supposed revision process. The poet's 'final version', which Root took to be represented by certain MSS, he termed 'β'. But for Root the readings of the remaining group represented the testimony of some corrupt and 'unauthorized' parent MS, which had 'escaped' at a point in the poem's revision before the state represented by Root's 'β' MSS had been reached. With an unhappy illogicality the text of this group – supposedly between 'α' and 'β' – was termed 'γ' by Root.

For Robinson[2] the MSS also indicated the existence of an earlier version, and he too considered that there were two groups among the other MSS. But he was unmoved by Root's argument that 'β' was the poet's final version, and dismisses it in one line of his Introduction. 'These readings (of 'β') appear . . . to be rather scribal than authoritative' (p. xl). Robinson consequently prefers the readings of 'γ' for his own edition, and his main argument with Root concerns the relative status of readings in 'γ' and 'β'. Yet Brusendorff[3] in his brief discussion of the same material, while apparently acknowledging the existence of an earlier version within the MSS, can conclude that the other variations are the work of careless copyists who misunderstood corrections in their exemplar.

The *Troilus* MSS produce evidence within themselves of certain groups of relatedness between MSS, but modern advances in textual criticism have modified the confidence of editors of Middle English texts both in traditional methods of recension and in other alternatives.[4] Root's approach to the *Troilus* MSS is confused by his confusion of manuscript traditions of the text with authorial versions of the poem, and by his attempt to arrange the manuscript families to represent successive authorial developments of the poem.[5] But whether these various scribal traditions of copying the poem in the *Troilus* MSS can also be seen to represent different approaches by the author to his material, distinct in time, style, or theme, needs very careful examination of the evidence.

I

Let us first examine what evidence the extant MSS give that there was a distinct earlier version of the *Troilus*, which Chaucer then went on to revise into the poem's familiar form. All the completed MSS present the poem in its five-book structure, and any signs of possible revision lie within that structure. Evidence for an earlier version is of two main types. There are certain 'large-scale' differences, where some MSS lack passages contained by the other MSS and where some MSS have passages in a rather different order. By contrast, the other type of evidence can be distinguished as 'small-scale', consisting of differences between MSS which are confined to a line or less of the poem.

The large-scale differences between some Ph*etc* MSS and the other MSS will be considered first. The disputed passages are Troilus's song in Book III (1744–71), his 'predestination soliloquy' in Book IV (953–1085), and his ascent to the spheres in Book V (1807–27). Certain of these passages are absent from some of the Ph*etc* MSS. But not all the passages are absent in all of the MSS normally holding with the Ph*etc* group at those points in the poem.

If passages are absent from certain MSS yet present in others it is possible to suppose this represents evidence for an authorial addition. But this interpretation of the MSS will depend on whether a viable text is presented without the disputed passages. Depending on the context, the same evidence for authorial addition may turn out to be evidence of scribal omission. The absence of the hero's song in Book III from some Ph*etc* MSS gives no clear support for the identity of a distinct earlier version of *Troilus*, either in the nature of the manuscript support or in the context of the disputed passage. Of the MSS normally agreeing with Ph in this part of the poem only one MS (H₂) in its completed form actually omits the song. The song has been added separately into Ph in the correction of the MS. The other Ph*etc* MSS (Gg H5) contain the passage normally. But the nature of the passage itself can explain its absence from some MSS. The material of Troilus's song has been added here by Chaucer from Boethius, in place of Troiolo's corresponding song in *Filostrato*. Chaucer had already used this Italian song selectively in his third proem, so that he needed material to replace it at the close of the third book if he wished to retain – as he did – the scene of the hero singing to Pandarus. That Chaucer always intended that his hero sing a song at this point is at least as sure as the unanimous testimony of the surviving MSS. For in the last line before the disputed song all extant MSS read 'And thanne he wolde synge in this manere' (1743).[6] It is then scarcely surprising that Gg includes the song and that the Ph scribe added it to his copy – for the simple reason that the context is, and must always have been, utter nonsense without it. Granted this, it is unhelpful of

4

Root to conclude: 'It seems clear that Chaucer's text existed for a time without the Boethian hymn to love' (*TT*, p. 157). What may survive at this point is a randomly preserved trace of the processes of Chaucer's composition of the poem. For the omission by some MSS precisely concerns a passage where Chaucer was making an intrusion into the sequence of his main narrative source and casting around for alternative material to *in-eche*. Such an expansion perhaps existed originally in the form of a physical addition to the draft which has been confused by certain scribes. Chaucer's working draft may well have been confusing here. But the sense of the context shows that no text of the poem could ever have been considered as completed and authentic without the Boethian stanzas of Troilus's song.

The Boethian song contains four stanzas, and is thus very comparable in size as a feature of the MSS with the absence from certain MSS of the three stanzas describing Troilus's ascent to the spheres (V, 1807–27). Chaucer borrows these stanzas from *Il Teseida*, inserting them into his translation of *Filostrato* at this point. Again, there is no distinct identity for a separate earlier version of the poem either in manuscript support for the absence of the stanzas, or in the literary quality of the context without the *Teseida* passage. Only one of the three Ph*etc* MSS at this part of the text actually omits this passage at all. This is Ph itself and (as with the song in Book III) the stanzas have been added to the MS. The two other Ph*etc* MSS here (H$_3$ and J) contain the passage normally. But two other MSS (H$_2$ and H$_4$) normally agreeing with R*etc* do *not* contain the passage. Such features of the MSS are more complex than can readily be explained by theories of a linear progression of authorial revision represented in the extant MSS. For here some MSS of Root's 'earliest' version contain the 'added' passage, while two MSS of what is supposedly the author's final and 'revised' text omit the passage which Chaucer has introduced into his main source.

Root's response to these features of the MSS is to accept as authentic only the evidence of Ph, while variously denigrating as scribal the peculiarities of H$_3$ and H$_2$H$_4$ (*TT*, p. 247). But Root's reasons for seeing the readings of these MSS here as the work of scribes can equally convincingly be applied to explain the nature of Ph itself. If H$_2$H$_4$ show how a scribe overlooked a passage on a loose leaf, then there is no reason to see the absence of the passage from Ph itself as having any further significance either. The evidence of the MSS does not indicate a distinct earlier version of the poem, valid without the *Teseida* stanzas. The confusion among the MSS suggests muddle by early scribes over a passage which was perhaps available to them separately because it did not form part of the author's main source.

The context shows that these stanzas were always to be included where they occur, between Chaucer's translations of *Fil.* 8.27 and 28. For Chaucer's adaptations of 8.28 imply that the *Teseida* stanzas have gone before. Boccaccio's dismissive tone ('il mal concetto amore di Troiolo') is adapted into exclamations on the hero's worth (1828–9) which – by lamenting this 'false worldes brotelnesse' (1832) – implicitly contrast this world and the next world where Troilus has gone. But one particular alteration to *Filostrato* proves that Chaucer always visualized the *Teseida* stanzas here. The Italian exclaims upon the end of Troiolo's bright splendour, worthy of a royal throne ('cotal fine ebbe il lucido splendore / che lui servava al solio reale'). But this Chaucer adapts to:

> *Swich fyn hath his estat real above.*
> (V, 1830)

Chaucer here alters his source so as to imply the presence of the *Teseida* stanzas, for the reference to Troilus's 'estat real *above*' can have no relation to anything that has gone before, except to the hero's ascent to the spheres, and would be a nonsense if it followed immediately on the simple report of his death.

The absence of these stanzas from some MSS is consequently more likely to stem from scribal omission than from subsequent authorial addition to a text which could have a prior independent existence without the passage. Like the song of Troilus, the passage was certainly added in the composition but not necessarily, indeed improbably, in a revision.

The song and the ascent of Troilus resemble the many other additions in the poem of reflective and 'philosophical' material which are all equally 'additions' to the story-line of *Troilus* as a *translacioun* of *Filostrato*, but are all equally demanded by their contexts. Criseyde's Boethian soliloquy in Book III (813–40), like that of Troilus in Book IV, very probably started life as an added sheet incorporated into Chaucer's narrative. But Criseyde's soliloquy is not taken as sign of a later, augmented version of the poem, because the extant MSS all happen to have correctly included that passage at its place in the text.

The absence from some MSS of Troilus's 'predestination soliloquy' in Book IV is the most bulky and most striking single difference among the manuscript groups. The soliloquy has been inserted into the middle of a single *Filostrato* stanza (4.109) which Chaucer breaks off, but to which he then returns and resumes translating after the soliloquy is complete. The rather ungainly quality of the passage, and a sense that it has not been well fitted to its context, have helped support the assumption that its absence from some MSS shows it was added by the poet as an afterthought to a pre-existing poem. But that the passage is 'added' (i.e. added to *Filostrato*) and that it is 'philosophical' in tone does not necessarily prove that it is 'later'.

The evidence of the MSS is particularly intricate:

1. H_3 and Ph do not contain 953–1085 (but it is added separately in Ph).
2. H_3Ph have a variant form and order for 950–52, not found in other MSS.
3. Gg omits all of the soliloquy, except the last stanza (1079–85) which is not derived from Boethius with the rest of the passage.
4. J – which holds with Ph*etc* from early in Book IV – *contains* the passage, *but* between the main soliloquy and that final stanza (1079–85) which Gg contains, there is a blank page, a cancelled leaf, and another blank space. At the foot of the last written page, *after* the main body of the soliloquy, is a scribal note: 'her faileth thyng yt is nat yt made'.
5. H_4 – which does not at this point normally agree with Ph*etc* – omits 953–1085 without any break in the text.

Once again, there is no cohesive, consistent manuscript support for the independent entity of an earlier version of the text. Once more, the context in all extant MSS indicates that the poem is unlikely to have been regarded as authentically completed without the predestination passage. Among the MSS, Ph itself is again at the heart of the variation in omitting the soliloquy from the main sequence of its text, as it does the song and the ascent, although all have then been added by the same scribe. H_3 omits the soliloquy, but contains the song and the ascent. Gg omits the soliloquy but contains the song (its text being lacking after V, 1701). J contains both the soliloquy and the ascent (it is not part of Ph*etc* in Book III). The H_4 omission of the soliloquy recalls the H_2H_4 agreement over the ascent, but this time H_2 does not agree.

Particularly revealing are the differences between the MSS near the beginning and end of the soliloquy, where it is fitted into its context in the poem. For Root the characteristics of H_3Ph, of Gg, and of J, are stages in an evolutionary process by which an earlier version is revised into a later more philosophical one ('We must distinguish three stages', *TT*, p. 219). To Root the variant lines in H₃Ph show a stage of Chaucer's text before the soliloquy is included in it. The characteristics of Gg and J are scribal reflections of a state of the text copied before its revision. In order to locate Gg on a line between H₃Ph and J, Root even asserts that it is characteristic that Chaucer would begin to compose an inserted passage from the end backwards (*TT*, p. 219). The confusions of J are interpreted as scribal reaction to an exemplar which had been copied with spaces left for material not yet completed by the revising poet. In brief, Root is concerned to see the MSS as evidence that Chaucer's text existed initially without the soliloquy.

Since Chaucer interpolates this enormous soliloquy into a single *Filostrato* stanza, it would not be surprising if the poet's own working draft did not read on completely smoothly from his *Filostrato*-based *translacioun* to the Boethian soliloquy and then back again. The soliloquy was for the poet an altogether different exercise in composition from the surrounding material. He was translating his stanzaic Italian source, but also including at a point within it a long section which he needed to versify into stanzas, probably working largely from his own prose *Boece*. It would not be unlikely if the long soliloquy were actually put together as an exercise separately and then married to the draft, always with the consequent possibility of scribal misinterpretation.

But however the omission of the soliloquy occurred, the varying readings in the MSS over the beginning and end of the soliloquy are united in indicating that at any stage of composition represented by the extant MSS, Chaucer intended the predestination soliloquy to be present in his poem. In the *Filostrato* stanza which Chaucer takes as his point of departure Pandaro simply finds Troiolo thoughtful and downcast in appearance ('pensoso e sì forte nel viso sbigottito', 4.109). But in Chaucer's translation, in all MSS, Pandarus finds Troilus alone in the temple, no longer caring for his life and making his moan to 'the pitouse goddes' (949). All extant MSS suggest Chaucer always conceived of his hero concerned here with questions of man's life and death and his relation to the gods. For the last three lines of this stanza H₃Ph differ somewhat in phrasing from the other MSS. Thus in H₃Ph, to the 'pitouse goddes':

> *He fast made his compleynt & his mone*
> *Bysekyng hem to sende hym oþir grace*
> *Or from þis world to done hym sone to pace*

In H₃Ph the soliloquy does not now follow. But in the other MSS these lines read:

Ful tendrely he preyed and made his mone
To doon hym sone oute of this worlde to pace
For wel he thoughte ther was non other grace.

The differences between H₃Ph and the others are not very substantial, but both readings may be authentic. The significant difference lies in the first line, where in most MSS Troilus tenderly prays, whereas in H₃Ph 'He fast made his compleynt'. Now although the soliloquy does not follow on to this in H₃Ph, it is precisely in the soliloquy that Chaucer's hero proceeds to make 'hys compleynt'. The H₃Ph lines imply the existence of the soliloquy in Chaucer's conception of the poem. Even if they do not contain the hero's 'compleynt' in its formulated shape, they insist more explicitly than the other MSS that this is the action in which Troilus is engaged at this point.

Chaucer's handling of the remainder of the interrupted Italian stanza, where the end of the soliloquy is connected back into the narrative, can also be seen to imply the presence of the Boethian passage. In *Filostrato*, when Pandaro finds Troiolo 'pensoso' he simply asks him whether he is as miserable as he appears ('or se' tu sì 'nvilito / come tu mostri?'). But in Chaucer's version Pandarus not only expresses himself much more urgently, but his urgency seems provoked in response to something he has just seen and heard ('O myghty God . . . in trone / I! who say evere a wis man faren so? / Whi, Troilus, what thinkestow to doone? / Hastow swich lust to ben thyn owen fo?' 1086–9). This strong response – present in all MSS – implies that Troilus is in a much more desperate state than in *Filostrato*. Yet without the presence of the soliloquy there is nothing to suggest that this is so or to draw such a response from Pandarus.

The peculiar evidence in Gg – also towards the end of the soliloquy – similarly indicates that the soliloquy was always to be present. For although Gg does not contain those stanzas actually translated from Boethius but only Chaucer's own last transitional stanza (1079–85), that last stanza explicitly describes the English Pandarus interrupting Troilus 'while he was in al this hevynesse / Disputyng with hymself in this matere' (1083–4). Although in Chaucer the Italian hint that Troiolo is 'pensoso' has become the hero's prayers, only the soliloquy shows him disputing with himself. As it stands the account given by Gg is nonsense, and cannot be other than scribal. It contains Chaucer's

9

changes to prepare his context, while lacking the very material which all these changes are designed to accommodate.

It is only by ignoring the very unequal merits and sense of the Ph *etc* readings in context that they can be taken to reflect a successive authorial revision of a text which is already being copied. For Root, after the H₃Ph stage, 'it then occurred to Chaucer to give to Troilus . . . a Boethian discussion of free choice and necessity' (*TT*, p. 219), and the Gg and J parents were derived at some stage before this process of revision was complete and so reflect the gaps in the author's draft. But granted their very inferior sense, it is at least equally plausible that Gg and J do not represent stages of a revision *in medias res*, so much as scribal misunderstandings *after the event* of the layers of composition present in a confusing exemplar, of which loose sheets may always have been lost.

The situation in J is baffling, but bafflingly scribal in quality: the soliloquy might have been invisibly incorporated into this text or its parent, if too much space had not been left. But if a scribe had a defective exemplar lacking the soliloquy he might well leave too much space for it, which would still be apparent after a complete exemplar had been acquired and the passage written in. For Root the scribal note in J ('her faileth thyng yt is nat yt made', f. 84ʳ) reflected a state of the text when scribes were waiting for Chaucer to complete his revision by composing the soliloquy. Yet this scribal note comes *after* the soliloquy as it occurs in J, and not *before* it, as would be necessary if it really stemmed from scribes who were close to the poet and who understood what he was doing. As it is, the note is suspiciously like a scribal guess at rationalizing a strange gap in an exemplar which there was no way of filling. It is unlikely to be authentic in suggesting – as it does in its location – that Chaucer was intending to translate more of the Boethius than he actually does. The position of the note contradicts its ostensible claim to be close to Chaucer's own intentions in composition.

Whatever the scribal interferences which have produced some distinctions between the frequently confused Ph *etc* MSS, the distinctions from the source in all extant MSS indicate that it is very unlikely that Chaucer ever intended the poem to have any completed 'published' existence without the Boethian passage. Indeed, without the soliloquy which so affects the overall philosophical tone of the whole poem there would have been less aptness in Chaucer's addressing the poem to 'Philosophical' Strode, a dedication present in all MSS. Without this, and the other omitted passages, it was less likely that Thomas Usk would call Chaucer 'the noble philosophical poete in Englissh'. For Love claims to Usk in his *Testament of Love* that it is precisely in *Troilus* that Chaucer reconciles God's prescience with man's free-will: in the *Troilus* Chaucer 'hath this mater touched and at the ful this questyon assoyled'.[7]

<h2 style="text-align:center">II</h2>

Most other evidence in the MSS for distinct states of the text is confined to much smaller-scale variations between the manuscript groups, consisting of differences over single words and phrases, variations of often less than a whole line. Root contended that his 'α' grouping preserves Chaucer's first and unrevised text, distinguished from the other MSS by readings which were closer to the Italian source, and also by readings which were 'earlier' in a creative process than the readings of the rest.

The evidence for a sustainedly distinct version or state of Chaucer's text, earlier and closer line by line to the Italian source, does not exist. What the MSS do contain is not so much any extended passages closer to the Italian, but some scattered points where the Ph*etc* MSS are demonstrably closer in word or phrase to the *Filostrato* original for that line, while the other *Troilus* MSS also contain an apparently authentic reading. Thus, for IV, 246–7, Ph*etc*, read:

> *His eyen too . . .*
> *So wepyn þat þei semyn wellis twey,*

while for the parallel line *Filostrato* has 'Forte piangeano e parean due fontane' (4.28). But the other MSS offer an equally authentic, indeed 'harder', reading:

> *Out stremeden as swifte welles tweye.*

The resemblance in sense and syntax of the Ph*etc* MSS to the Italian source, and the authenticity of the other *Troilus* reading are equally clear. In such a line, the Ph*etc* MSS, by whatever means of transmission, suggest their sporadic links with the poet's own composition. A scattering of such instances – of very varying quality – marks Book I and part of III and IV. In few of these instances is there any very marked identity to either the Ph*etc* reading or that of the others. If the Ph*etc* readings do reveal points where Chaucer has altered his first thoughts in composition, they do not concern signal points of characterization or event, but points of expression, suggesting how Chaucer has moved away from his source. This can be seen in the variants for I, 83, 85:

Fil. 1.9   da lui sperando sommo e buon consiglio
Ph etc   Hopyng in hym kunnyng hem to rede (I, 83)
Rest   In trust that he hath konnynge hem to rede (I, 83)

Fil. 1.10   Fu'l romor grande quando fu sentito
Ph etc   Grete rumour was whan hit was ferst aspyed (I, 85)
Rest   The noise vp ros whan it was first aspied (I, 85)

In some cases the resemblance in Ph*etc* to *Filostrato* presents a reading rather harder, because more Latinate, than that of the other MSS. At least in some such cases the reading further from the Italian is possibly scribal, and the same holds for the many instances throughout the poem where the *other* MSS are closer to the Italian than Ph*etc*. In yet other cases, context and theme allow that the closer approximation to Italian in some MSS is possibly coincidental.

However, the relatively few instances where there are two convincing readings for a line offer an intriguing glimpse into the process of the poem's composition, as with one rare case of variation extending over more than a single line, in which Ph*etc* shows itself closer to *Filostrato*. In *Troilus* Book IV, one stanza (ll. 750–6 in Robinson's edition) is copied in Ph*etc* in a sequence which corresponds to the order of the parallel stanzas in *Filostrato*, while the other MSS have the stanza in a different, but equally authentic, ordering. (By citing here the first three lines of the disputed stanza and the first lines of the other three stanzas involved, the differences between Ph*etc* and the other MSS in this description of Criseyde's woe can be brought out schematically.) First the situation as it exists in Ph*etc* (here Gg, H₃, J, Ph):

A. *The salt teris from her eyen tweyne*
    Out ran as shour in Aprill ful swithe;
    Her white brest she bet & for þe peyne . . .

B. *Her ownded here þat sunnisshe was of hewe . . .* (Ph *ornyd*)

C. *'Alas,' quod she, 'out of this regioun . . .'*

D. *'What shal y done, what shal he done also . . .'*

Now the situation as found in all other MSS:

B. *Hire ownded heer that sonnysshe was of hewe* . . .   (736 ff.)

C. *'Allas,' quod she* . . . etc

A. *Therwith the teris from hire eyen two*
   Down fille as shoure in April (ful) swithe;
   Hire white brest she bette and for the wo . . .

D. *She seyde, 'How shal he don and ich also?'*

The order of the descriptive details in Ph*etc* does follow more closely
the order of the source. In the first stanza Criseyde weeps and beats
her breast (cf. 'piangendo sì forte . . . e'l bianco petto / spesso
batteasi', 4.87/2–4). In the second stanza she tears her hair (cf. 'e'
biondi crin tirandosi rompea', 4.87/7). In stanzas C and D she
laments, in direct speech, that she must depart. But in the other MSS
Criseyde's tearing of her hair is moved to become her first response,
with the effect that the description of unhappiness is interspersed with
Criseyde's laments, and her tears follow on to her first exclamations.
Both Stanzas A and D have been adapted for different contexts, and
the rhymes of the disputed stanza undergo minor change.

But although Ph*etc* is closer to the source in the sequence of some
descriptive details, other phrases in the passage show some of that
inappropriateness and inferiority more generally characteristic of
Ph*etc*.

All the MSS agree that Chaucer always intended to compare the
profusion of Criseyde's tears to an April shower (751). But in Ph*etc*,
although the tears are described as a shower, they only *out ran*,
whereas the other MSS – by telling how the tears *doun fille* – present
the idea fully worked out. Again, when Criseyde curses the day she
first saw Troilus, she says in the other MSS 'Wo worth allas that ilke
dayes light' (747). But in Ph*etc* she declares rather feebly: 'Wo worth
þat day (and) namly that night'. Ph*etc* seems clichéd, and less precise
and appropriate to context. Chaucer perhaps translated and versified
these stanzas first in the Italian order and indicated the change of
sequence in his margin, a direction then lost in some MSS. For the
poor quality of some readings, adjacent in the text to others which
apparently go back to Chaucer's first translation of the Italian,
suggests that this is the survival, possibly corrupted, of a rough early
draft.

This is also the impression made more generally by the readings
closer to *Filostrato* in Ph*etc* and the way they survive: isolated points of
resemblance to the source, scattered in the MSS among many inferior

variations of scribal quality. The same can be said of variations between the MSS over the poem's classical allusions. At a few points Ph*etc* may preserve traces of the poet's composition process, as when (at IV, 644) Ph*etc* has Pandarus ask Troilus how he can know Criseyde's opinion:

> *But eny Aungill told hit in thi ere?* (Ph þe hit)

The other MSS read:

> *But if that Ioue told it in thyn ere?*

Yet individual scribes in the *Troilus* MSS can elsewhere be observed to remove pagan references: for IV, 1149 ('O Ioue I deye and mercy I beseche') the scribe of Ad reads 'O Syon I deye . . .'. In most cases of variation over classical readings the Ph*etc* reading seems scribally inferior.

Resemblances to Italian and variations over Classical references are among the few aspects of variation in Ph*etc* to which a decided character can be given. Most variation is characterizable only at the level of some recurrent differences in related types of diction and in simpler syntactical patterns.[8] At this level, variations are characterizable almost in proportion as they are more likely to be scribal than authentic. It is overwhelmingly through such intrinsically indifferent variation that Ph*etc* differentiates itself from the other MSS. With Ph*etc* the true extent and quality of the evidence for a distinct authorial earlier version must be distinguished from the momentum which Root's presentation and description may give it. For it is an essential feature of Root's approach that if some readings in a group are judged authentic then all variations in that group can be seen in the light of possible authenticity. But in the circumstances of scribal copying there is no necessary reason why some authentic readings need endow any others with authority, simply because they occur in the same manuscript family. Authority can only be relative among the MSS in each reading, especially in MSS like those of *Troilus*, where parts of extant MSS are copied by different hands from different exemplars. The precise identity of the MSS which are held to support Root's 'α' alters repeatedly through the poem, so that the editorial conception of an identity for an 'α' version is much more consistent than the support of the MSS themselves.

It is important to distinguish the consistency that may mark scribal agreements between a group from the agreements which may distinguish that manuscript group as also representing an authentic state of the text. What the Ph*etc* MSS largely present is the character of a manuscript group, not a 'version' of the text. To all intents and purposes the Ph*etc* family has no identity which is anything other than scribal, except in certain parts of Books I, III and IV. Here, it sporadically produces some fascinating readings. But these should be seen with the implications of their isolation and scribal context rather than allowed to endow their manuscript family as a whole with an interest of possible authenticity throughout the poem which in themselves the run of variants cannot support.

III

Its persistent scribal variations set off the Ph*etc* MSS markedly from the other MSS, but distinctions between these remaining MSS also exist – although of a very different type and extent from the readings in Ph*etc*. It is these distinctions between Cp*etc* and R*etc* which have been seen to mark two successive stages of Chaucer's poem after Ph*etc* in time: Root's 'β', or the poet's final revision, and 'γ', an unauthorized text of the *Troilus* between 'α' and 'β'. A conception of the groups as reflecting a progressive authorial revision process depends on Root's characterization of his 'γ' group as being 'midway' between the states of the text he finds represented by his 'α' and 'β'. But there is no satisfactory evidence that Root's 'γ' is midway between 'α' and 'β'. There are no firm grounds in the MSS for seeing the readings of the Cp*etc* and R*etc* groups in any authentic progressive ordering as separate 'versions' of the text.

Root's view of his 'γ' as between 'α' and 'β' is based on two types of evidence. Firstly, he accepts as authentic all the three readings in those very rare and scattered instances in the poem where all three manuscript groups present a distinct account of the same line. Secondly, although Root generally finds his 'γ' and 'β' agreeing together as against 'α', for some time in Book III he finds his 'α' and 'γ' agreeing as against 'β'. This feature is taken to show that 'γ' was derived before Book III had been revised, although it was derived late enough to share many other 'β' readings elsewhere in the poem (*TT*, p. 252).

But the argument for a sustained authorial involvement with the poem through several 'versions' or successive editions survives with difficulty any examination of the nature and quality of the detailed

15

variants on which these supposed 'versions' have to be built. Thus, where Cp*etc* and R*etc* vary from each other in Book III, in almost every case one of the variants on one side or the other is demonstrably inferior, and probably scribal.[9] There is no convincing evidence here for seeing Cp*etc* or R*etc* as wholes in a necessarily successive sequence of revision. Neither of these groups has a monopoly of authority. Again, in most cases where there is a three-way division of readings for one line between the three groups, at least one of the readings, and often two, can be seen to be probable scribal variants of the other.[10] That the three-way divisions usually involve this kind of material simply contradicts the over-interpretation of suggesting they support the identity of three distinct authorial versions of the text. Both manuscript groups have sporadic claims to authenticity, but the few impressive distinctions between Cp*etc* and R*etc* are widely scattered, and contrast with the much more persistent character-in-variation of both groups as the outcomes of separate scribal traditions of copying the poem.

These relative claims to authenticity can be seen in several of the variants of the R*etc* group. In Book III two stanzas (ll. 1324–37 in Robinson) occur in a different position in R*etc* than in the other MSS. In these stanzas the narrator puts his 'wordes heere and every part' under the correction of those 'that felyng han in loves art'. The two stanzas are found in R*etc* (and in H_3 and S_1, both often associated with R) between ll. 1414 and 1415 (in Robinson's line-numbering).

The case for the authenticity of the stanzas as located in R*etc* is weaker on contextual grounds, as can be seen by comparing the stanzas which precede and follow the disputed stanzas in their two positions in the MSS. In the other MSS, these stanzas – concerned with the suitability of language used by an inexperienced narrator – are preceded by two stanzas explicitly concerned with the inadequate powers of the poet ('But juggeth ye that han ben at the feste . . . I kan namore' (1312–4); 'this hevene blisse . . . that is so heigh that al ne kan I telle' (1323)). By contrast, in the R*etc* MSS the stanzas are not preceded by stanzas concerned with expression at all. We hear that the lovers' speech is usually broken up by kissing (1403) and that they pass their nights 'in joie and bisynesse / Of al that souneth into gentilesse' (1413–4). It is now in the R*etc* MSS that the poet apologizes for his inexperience. There is nothing positively inappropriate in this, but nor do the stanzas have any special attachment and continuity in this later position, as they do in the earlier.

The stanzas which *follow* the disputed stanzas in each of their positions again show that the position in the other MSS than R*etc* has positive advantages in connectedness. For the two disputed stanzas acknowledge themselves in their (undisputed) last line to be a digression ('But now to purpos of my rather speche', 1337). In their earlier position in the text these stanzas do interrupt what seems a continuity of attention to the lovers at their consummation. The stanza which here follows them opens by acknowledging some intervention ('Thise ilke two that ben in armes laft', 1338). This is more likely to refer to 1324–37 than to 1317–23, and has been adapted from *Filostrato* ('Ei non uscir di braccio l'uno all'altro', 3.34) so as to imply interruption. By contrast, the stanza which follows in R*etc* has no relation to the disputed stanzas and contradicts their claim to be returning 'to purpos of my rather speche' by promptly introducing a new subject. For there now follows the dawn and the lovers' sadness (1415 ff.), whereas the poem has so far only mentioned their joy in 'this nyght that was to hem so deere' (1411). Some variant readings in the stanzas and in adjacent lines in R*etc* are not beyond scribal work. In brief, the stanzas can stand in either position without absolute incongruity. But as a self-conscious digression on art they are much more contextually implied, and thus more effective, in their earlier position. There remains little positive evidence that the different location of these stanzas in R*etc* represents authentic revision when the divergence between the MSS may be compared with a number of bizarre scribal errors by copyists in the *Troilus* MSS, where stanzas are misplaced. H_4 carries these disputed stanzas twice, copying them out in *both* positions (H_4, f. 75^v and f. 77^r). In a probably less conscious shifting of material in R itself, five stanzas are copied out twice at different positions within Book III (ll. 1212–46 occur between 1099 and 1100 (f. 54^v–f. 55) and in their proper place (f. 57^r–f. 57^v)).

With these disputed stanzas there appears neither equality nor discernible progression between the variations, while the other evidence of the same MSS shows comparable interference by their scribes. But there remain limited cases where the R*etc* MSS do represent an apparent progression in difficulty beyond the authentic readings of the other MSS, and an interesting instance occurs early in Book IV. Now there are several cases (undisputed textually) where the English poet has evidently corrected his Italian source over matters of 'historical' detail where he found Boccaccio differed from Benoit and Guido. In IV, 51, Chaucer contradicts *Filostrato* (4.3) by introducing the word *maugre* which reverses the Italian sense. (In

Filostrato Polidamas and the other listed Trojans are all captured along with Antenor, but there was no authority for this in Benoit and Guido.) In IV, 138, by the mention of King Thoas, or in V, 1038, by mentioning the captured horse, Chaucer is supplementing Boccaccio from Benoit and Guido. Given this larger tendency to 'correct' *Filostrato*, it is intriguing to find a dispute between the *Troilus* MSS at a point where there is such a dispute between Boccaccio and Benoit. In IV, 57–9, the variants in both R*etc* and Cp*etc* equally contradict *Filostrato* which says Priam asked for a truce (4.4). In R*etc* and the other MSS the Greeks ask for the truce, and the English variants could indicate that Chaucer returned to polish up his emendation of 'fact'.[11]

However, this type of specific, harder reading carries a conviction of authenticity which most readings of the R*etc* group do not have. Few such vigorously characterized differences distinguish R*etc* from Cp*etc*, but where they do exist they may reflect some spasmodic authorial tinkering with an established MS. It is not unlikely that Chaucer would occasionally modify his poem in a copy that was to hand, especially tidying up the occasional point of 'fact'. But generally Cp*etc* and R*etc* do not identify themselves from each other in anything more than their own internal errors as manuscript groups. Interesting distinctions between them exist very occasionally, within a continuum of minor divergence in vocabulary and phrasing which is more likely to reflect their transmission through different scribal traditions than to represent an authorial rewriting so indifferent and motiveless as to be distinguished with difficulty from the more generally observable characteristics of scribal copying.

IV

These sporadic instances of authenticity in a manuscript family are part of a wider pattern in the *Troilus* MSS, which present some baffling instances of striking independence by individual MSS or groupings. These make difficult the interpretation of the *Troilus* MSS as they stand as presenting evidence for successive, distinct authorial versions of the poem. Thus, at the end of part III of *Filostrato* Boccaccio leaves his hero in joy and felicity, but warns in the last stanza (3.94) of the deceit and animosity of Fortune. The Ph*etc* and R*etc* MSS show that Chaucer has altered the disposition of the material, so that the third book ends with Troilus in joy, and the fourth proem opens with warnings of Fortune's enmity. But in some Cp*etc* MSS the third book is not marked to end until *after* the warnings of the fourth proem on Fortune, which is thus included in the third book.[12] In brief, some Cp*etc* MSS (Root's 'midway' version) have the text in a state closest here to the Italian source. It is improbable that any truly 'midway' state of the text between the earlier, 'more Italian' version, and the final 'revision' of a successively revised poem would have a feature of the source possessed by neither of the other 'versions'. The resemblance to *Filostrato* depends on rubrication and so could be due to scribal confusion. But this remains a fascinating case of the 'unauthorized' text of Root's theory apparently preserving a line right back to a moment of decision in the author's composition process.

There is comparably baffling peculiarity among the R*etc* MSS, in R itself. R has a special interest in that it contains as well as *Troilus* the only extant text of Chaucer's *To Rosemounde*. In *Troilus* R also contains a stanza – of apparently authentic versification and diction – found in no other MS.[13] This R stanza is comparable with the stanza contained by the Ph*etc* MSS but by no others (I, 890–96), and is possibly an isolated 'spot' survival of a stanza cancelled in Chaucer's composition process. There are unsatisfactory features to the stanza suggesting it is not part of an authentic finalized text. Yet the association in R with the authoritative survival of *Rosemounde*, one of the poet's short lyrics, could indicate that this stanza is an authentic part of the poet's composition. But however tantalizing the existence of this solitary stanza, there is something even more peculiar in R. This MS does not contain the proems to Books II, III and IV. Again, in Book V, R and H$_4$ alone of all the MSS do not contain the Latin summary of Statius (after V, 1498). It is difficult to locate the evidence of R as a whole before or after the features in other MSS as representing one stage in a process of authorial revision. R has been thought part of the author's final 'version', yet it is inconceivable that Chaucer should cancel the proems at some later stage, when they form so important a part of the balance of his poem. The omission of the proems compares with the omitted passages in Ph*etc*, also authorial elaborations of the narrative line provided by *Filostrato*. Their omission may represent early scribal confusion over the inclusion of these extra-narrative passages. (Since the proems vary in length a physical cause like loss of leaves would not explain their absence.) The absence of the proems and the presence of the unique stanza show a MS which throughout its line-by-line texture presents a standard finished text, but which at isolated points seemingly contradicts that character and could reach back close to a compositional phase. Such momentary textual 'flash-backs', both in Cp*etc* and in R, suggest that among the *Troilus* MSS the various groups have an integrity as phenomena of scribal transmission, but that none of them has a consistent integrity throughout as being equivalent to a distinct state of the author's text, separate in time and conception from that represented by the other groups.[14]

The most rewarding lesson of the *Troilus* MSS is that the evidence should be seen as it is, and not distorted by comparisons with the models of revision in some other contemporary texts, or marshalled to fit uneasily with traditional ideas of manuscript descent. To recognize for itself the particular nature of the *Troilus* MSS can imply much more about the way this ambitious poem first came to exist and was first read. Within Chaucer's own works, the supposed instances of *Troilus* revision bear no relation to the principal case of Chaucer's extended rewriting, the Prologue to *The Legends of Good Women*. The Prologue presents sustained reworking of one continuous text into another, with changes in ideas, order of material, emphasis and tone. The two versions of the Prologue exist clearly separate in time as equally finished works, and the same can be said of the types of revision surviving in the MSS of Gower and Langland, yet all are quite distinct in kind from the evidence of the *Troilus* MSS.

In Gower's alterations of substantial blocks of material within the *Confessio Amantis* there might seem some resemblance to the differences over blocks of text in *Troilus*.[15] But the analogy is a deceptive one. The Gower MSS reflect close authorial overseeing with large-scale changes of chunks of text at different periods, which marked distinct editions of the *Confessio* as the author's interests changed with the times. Comparison – either close or general – with Langland's approach is also misleading for *Troilus*. Langland's compulsive revision sustained throughout the work produces a distinct three-stage development which superficially resembles Root's view of *Troilus*.[16] But again the comparison is a deceptive one, which distorts the nature and proportions of the *Troilus* evidence. The three versions of *Piers Plowman* are separate attitudes to a conception and as such exist distinctly and individually valid at different times. But the *Troilus* MSS do not divide among themselves in this way. Their evidence is better allowed to speak for itself than stretched by comparisons with

Gower's block-revision or Langland's three-fold progression which it cannot support. For the *Troilus* is either nonsense or impoverished without its 'blocks' (the song, the soliloquy, the ascent), and shows no sustained and motivated rewriting of form and content across a period of time and manuscript production, as does *Piers Plowman*.

The distinctions between the *Troilus* MSS are of a much quieter, more delicate nature, almost never so highly coloured as in these contemporary models of revision. By comparison with the distinguishable stages and published entities in time of Gower's and Langland's texts, most of the distinctions between the *Troilus* MSS give the impression of being curiously on top of one another, in both the temporal and spatial sense of the expression. Because their works were related to continuing developments in their times and beliefs, Gower and Langland were keeping their large poems open-ended during their lives. In the *Troilus*, any motives for revision are less distinct in time by being more stylistic and possibly intellectual than topical. There is little support from the *Troilus* MSS that clearly differentiated and self-sufficient versions of the poem existed at significantly distinct periods in time. The *Troilus* variations seem 'on top of one another' in time, in that the most striking differences – the absence of the philosophical passages – intrinsically disprove that they represent a completed authentic text. The *Troilus* variations seem on top of one another in space, in that those remaining distinctions between the MSS which are persuasively authorial in quality are also marked by the delicacy and limited scope of their character, as if they represent authentic but localized superimpositions on to an established text.[17]

To say that the *Troilus* existed for a while without its philosophical passages is comparable to saying that St Paul's Cathedral existed for a while without its dome, that is, until the plan implied by the rest of the structure was completed. If Gower's and Langland's MSS represent how those poets intended their work should be read by a public at various times, the *Troilus* MSS can reflect more intimately how the poem was written, and then how read by its scribes. The existence of traditions of scribal copying of the poem need not drive the temporal and material wedges of separate 'versions' or editions of the text between the superimposed layers of composition in the *Troilus*. The very notion of editions and versions draws a definiteness of identity and integrity from the world of print which is inapplicable to the age of manuscript, when the complete and material difference between a modern author's working drafts and his published appearance in print could be less distinct. There remains an intrinsic interest in the nature of the *Troilus* MSS, in that so ambitious a poem could survive in such a relatively casual state. But this is no more than is implied by Chaucer's own expressed anxiety about the fate of his poem in transmission (V, 1793–9) which suggests his mixture of apprehension and resignation that its form will very soon pass out of his control. The right to adapt was a defence against this during a poet's lifetime,[18] but not one Chaucer seems on the evidence to have used with any extensiveness or energy. Indeed, given the proven range of sources and incorporations which lie behind the poem, the great work of compilation and composition already accomplished in the text of all MSS is proportionately more striking in itself than the possible touches of further revision preserved in some MSS. Probably by scribal accident, the *Troilus* MSS preserve intriguing, isolated traces of the composition of this layered poem, and can suggest that the poet returned here and there to his text. Yet for Chaucer – as the evidence of the MSS embodies in itself – the great work was already done.

The Lesson of the *Troilus*: Chastisement and Correction

ALAN T. GAYLORD

> Pluralism and dualism are not, as we are frequently invited to
> believe, the final achievement in experience with regard to some
> ideas; they are characteristic of any world when insufficiently
> known. A diversity judged to be ultimate and unconditional is
> the form of all that fails to be satisfactory in experience.
>
> *Michael Oakeshott*[1]

I wish to account for the meaning of the *Troilus* by describing its
experience as a lesson. The end of the lesson is wisdom, which I take
to be a condition of emotional and intellectual satisfaction, a state of
rest after a struggle or a journey, and not a ranked series of axioms.
Hence, it will not do to describe the lesson as a moral *sentence*, set
down at one place. The ending of the *Troilus* is the end of the lesson;
one cannot pass the course, however, by reading it alone.

I do not speak of several, possibly contradictory, lessons. There is
not one lesson for Book I, another for Book III, and still another for
the Epilogue. The condition to be achieved is not only of wholeness,
but of self-conscious meditative repose, a return to the mirror after
gazing through the glass. The veil of fiction is parted, the exemplary
force of the narrative realized. If one has learned the lesson, one is
'daswed', and 'domb as any stoon'; if one has not learned the lesson,
one is restless, 'fulfyld of thought and busy hevynesse'.

The busy heaviness of the critics is, unfortunately, a matter of
record. As a group, we do not have 'that thyng' that we would.

Although any new remedy must also be part of the disease, I wish to argue against certain of our modern predilections which are in need of chastisement and correction. In their medieval and Chaucerian senses, these two terms may help bring us to rest.

In this essay, I will begin by identifying the major critical responses I find misleadingly 'modern'; then review the lesson of the *Troilus* as I think Chaucer arranges it; and then – since this is only a fraction of what a longer study could accomplish – I will discuss one example of frustrated chastisement within the poem; and will conclude with an analysis of Chaucer's final appeal for correction.

I

Chastisement in its medieval sense has at its root instruction, not punishment; as when Pandarus states that 'wyse ben by foles harm chastised' (III, 329).[2] Elsewhere, the Monk describes the hapless Seneca annoying Nero with virtuous counsel, 'for he fro vices wolde hym ay chastise' (B[2], 3695); and Boethius declares that good or evil Fortune is in part 'to punysschen or elles chastisen schrewes' (*Boece*, IV, pr 7) – where *chastisen* translates *corrigendi* from the Latin. Indeed, it will be seen that *chastisement* is itself a kind of correction, applied to the process of education and the development of thought. The two works that so substantially stand behind the *Troilus*, the *Roman de la Rose* and *The Consolation of Philosophy*, both deal with chastisement. The *Roman* may be seen as a succession of tutors, of whom the most splendid, Raison, is the only one who actually attempts to *chastier*, and is the only one who is absolutely rejected. For, as L'Amant says, 'Who that me chastiseth, I hym hate': 'Si n'aim mie qui me chastie'.[3] He will seek more complaisant instructors. It is as Raison sardonically observes: 'He is wis, that wol hymsilf chastyse' (3238), and the *Roman* adds 'E quant ieunes hons fet folie, / L'en ne se point merueillier' ('So when a young man acts foolishly, no one should be at all surprised', ll. 3016–7); that is, a young man, not being wise, had best not appoint himself as his own tutor. Yet it is L'Amant's alter ego, Bel Ami, who replaces Raison by validating and ministering to L'Amant's desires. In the *Troilus*, as I have argued elsewhere,[4] Raison never gets a chance to be heard directly, and Troilus undertakes his own instruction, in collusion with his Fair-Friend, Pandarus.

In the *Consolation*, chastisement meets with similar resistance at

24

first, but Lady Philosophy, as the Parson also urges, is 'war from chidynge or reprevynge' and thus is able to 'chastise with benignitee' and with an 'amyable tonge' ($627–8). The structure of the work is spiral, in the sense that simple conceptions are corrected into more complex, and naïve visions raised to higher understanding, while the same problems are reformulated at more precise levels of abstraction. It is important to note that this instruction, in good Platonic terms, teaches what is already known; the end of the lesson is recognition, based on recollection.

So, also, in the *Troilus*. The chastisement of the hero is tragicomically ineffectual. There is no one in the poem to correct him. And his final vision is more like a quick peek in the back of the book, than a completed lesson. He had not attended. He could not, even with the friends he had, learn what he needed.

At this point, whole colleges of critics recoil. They wish to give Troilus credit for trying. And they make their quarrel with what they take to be the lesson, which turns out to be one or all of the lines spoken by Chaucer at the end, especially

> *thynketh al nys but a faire*
> *This world, that passeth soone as floures faire.*
> (V, 1840–1)

It is lovely poetry, indeed, and affecting, and deserves examination and commentary. But remarking the *rime riche* of the couplet as an elegantly intensive rhetorical flourish (cf. General Prologue, A17–8), and understanding the thematic importance of 'faire' during its history through the *Troilus* – translating as it does the world's apparent beauty from such texts as the *Consolation* (*pulchrum*) and the *Roman* (*bel, biaus, Bel Semblant*), still does not convert a motif into a lesson. Just as Lady Philosophy had more to do than persuade Boethius he was a wretch, so is there more to learn in the *Troilus* than a melancholy hope and a spasmodic faith.

A great many able critics have gotten into trouble by first oversimplifying their definition of the lesson of the *Troilus*, and then overcomplicating their response to its effect. In so doing, they are 'correcting' Chaucer, but in a peculiar way. True, he seems to have prompted them:

> *For myne wordes, heere and every part,*
> *I speke hem alle under correccioun*
> *Of yow that felyng han in loves art.*
> (III, 1331–3)

25

And although the critics seldom respond as erotic specialists (for the original context is intensely 'Venerien'), they do display feelingly a love for the things of this world and a life amidst the flux, abounding in contraries. Thus if Chaucer says 'repeyreth hom fro worldly vanyte', and 'what nedeth feynede loves for to seke?' (V, 1837, 1848), he must surely have meant something else, and must be corrected.

E. T. Donaldson identifies the lesson as the *moralitee* of the poem: 'simply this: that human love, and by a sorry corollary everything human, is unstable and illusory'; but he goes on to insist that 'the meaning of the poem is not the moral, but a complex qualification of the moral'.[5] That, I take it, has become the motto of the modern critic as he 'corrects' Chaucer: *only complexly qualify.*

Troilus's fervent idealism is taken as the highest kind of human love. If nothing human can be perfect, Troilus has done the best that is humanly possible. And hence, as Alfred David argues, 'Troilus' tragic error, if such an error can be called tragic, is to have tried to love a human being with an ideal spiritual love'.[6] David's is perhaps the purest and most forceful instance of a critic combining a sympathetic reading of the central character with that New Critical yoking together of opposing values which Donaldson and Muscatine have made popular. Troilus is rescued from the moralists and defended as intelligent – in David's words, successfully, if painfully, 'searching out the universal meaning of his personal experience' (p. 568). Like Wolfram's Parzival, he is 'a brave man slowly wise'.[7] And so, David concludes, 'Troilus' celestial laughter recognizes at the same time the absurdity *and* the sublimity of human endeavor' (p. 580).

The 'absurdity' would seem to be based upon the presumed fact that Troilus cannot do any better than he does, that, beyond a certain point, he is powerless to make the rest of the world conform to his ideals. The late-century critics are thus modifying and amplifying Kittredge's stress upon the idea of 'compelling destiny', and his explication of 'the tragedy of character'. For example, in his edition of Chaucer, Donaldson tries to define the relationship which is established in the poem between character and fate:

> The impossibility of a human being's becoming anything but what he is is one of the principal points – perhaps the principal point – that the poem makes, and it is toward this point that the poem has been steadily moving. . . . Chaucer . . . presents in *Troilus and Criseyde* a pattern of human instability. Criseide is its chief exponent in terms of human character; Pandarus in terms

of human action. Troilus comes, because of his *trouthe*, as near to stability as man may come; but within a world where mutation is the law – and in a world in which the stability of a Christian god does not exist – it does him no good.[8]

One might say that this compassionate view epitomizes a tendency in modern criticism to correct the poem into an elegy, rather than a tragedy, and to stress the theme of mutability more than the principle of accountability. If the characters are only in part to be blamed, they are all the more to be pitied. Donaldson concludes:

> The simultaneous awareness of the real validity of human values – and hence our need to commit ourselves to them – and of their inevitable transitoriness – and hence our need to remain uncommitted – represents a complex, mature, truly tragic vision of mankind. (p. 980)

'Human values' seem to be the unchastised world of behavior enclosed by the *Troilus*, as if we had seen there the simple best of the Old World. The description leaves no room for alternatives other than other-worldliness. The attempt to soar into anagogy must be pulled back to little earth. This 'vision' is 'tragic' with a resonant, Arnoldian melancholy.[9] It circumscribes the small cosmos of Troilus's last vision, and transcends the necessity of choice through the embracing of paradox: *only complexly qualify*.

That is one line of modern correction. There is another. The first finds Chaucer's poem unified because its experience successfully denies little and affirms all. The second finds it dual, a testament to Chaucer's struggle with the dualism of his age. Within this line, critics find Chaucer correcting himself, rapt in his 'matere' and loath to go where it must take him. Perhaps the first significant voice here was that of C. S. Lewis, who gave us that brilliant image for the Epilogue taken as palinode: 'We hear the bell clang; and the children, suddenly hushed and grave, and a little frightened, troop back to their master.'[10] The greatest part of the poem is holiday, but we come back to 'master' because we must. As Elizabeth Salter extends the theme: '*Troilus* displays to us a poet whose gradually changing purposes involve him in greater and greater difficulty with his sources.'[11] Hence, in creating his own Criseyde, Chaucer must struggle against 'the sheer weight of substance of the original' (p. 94), and Book III is written 'in defiance of the known ending of the story' (p. 99). Books IV and V, then, 'record a gradual, difficult readjustment to authority. . . . The admirable recklessness of his actions has to be paid for' (p. 104). We are cautioned, as the bell sounds and the children troop back (sullenly, one supposes), that 'we should not mistake philosophic and religious reconciliation for imaginative committal', for 'the sad bewilderment with which Chaucer watches his poem shrink to a tale of treachery cannot be wholly remedied . . .' (p. 105).

Alfred David has adopted a similar view, in a more recent work: contradicting Kittredge, he asserts 'Chaucer in composing *Troilus* did *not* fully know what he was about and was a true Poet *because* of, not in spite of, this fact.'[12] And he adds, 'What I feel myself is a profound split on Chaucer's part between what his intellect as a medieval moralist tells him ideally should be and what his feelings as a poet tell him actually is true' (p. 30). By emphasizing 'poet' in this way, David illuminates what it is this line of critics are doing to correct the poem: Chaucer has become a proto-novelist, but with very modern neurotic apprehensions, struggling to free himself of his own work – like a spider trying to become a moth. So Salter writes, 'the unique excellence of *Troilus and Criseyde* is . . . to be counted . . . the growth and release of a poet's imagination' ('A Reconsideration', p. 88). And in so characterizing the poet, the critics have become onlookers more than readers, the text representing for them a history of the poet's struggle to remain true to his artistic self – a self presumed alienated from orthodoxy, medieval society, and moral philosophy.

'Clearly,' writes Salter in another study, 'acquiescence, the act of conformity to whatever is traditional and established, was an essential and quite natural part of Chaucer's make-up.'[13] The doubts that Chaucer expresses about his narrative, the loyalties he displays for his erring characters, the warmth he evinces for their passions – all these will be put aside when Master calls to prayers. It was the medieval way. Still, we may cherish the flashes of rebellion or originality, for 'we cannot be blamed if we still find that there are times when he writes about human beings as few other mediaeval poets did, with a freedom and understanding which reaches our sympathies at the highest imaginative level' (p. 70). This kidnapping of the poet to Wordsworthian heights represents the extreme version of modern critical correcting of a too-docile conventional poet. It leads me to recommend a return to Chaucer's own sense and usage, where *correccioun* relates rather to a reader's personal commitment to the lesson of the text, than to a critic's revision of that lesson to accord with modernist predilections.

To be sure, the call to 'correccioun' in the *Troilus* seems to make the audience, not the poet, the authority. Just as it is Chaucer's initial pose that he deals with matters his audience knows more about than he: 'Forwhi to every lovere I me excuse, / That of no sentement I this endite, / . . . Disblameth me, if any word be lame' (II, 12–3, 17); so is it his later pose that he must pray to others' gods for appropriate inspiration (III, 39–48), and seek others' approval for his speech:

> *And if that ich, at Loves reverence,*
> *Have any word in eched for the beste,*
> *Doth therwithal right as yourselven leste.*
>
> *For myne wordes, heere and every part,*
> *I speke hem alle under correccioun*
> *Of yow that felyng han in loves art. . . .*
> (III, 1328–33)

These are the lovers 'that ben in the cas / Of Troilus' (I, 29–30), and may take him as their mirror. Yet the question of relating to Troilus involves, throughout the poem, the matter of learning from his example. Those who correct only by confirming in him their ruling passions are overlooking the theme of exemplification, first stated by Troilus in disdain: 'O veray fooles, nyce and blynde be ye! / Ther nys nat oon kan war by other be' (I, 202–3); then repeated as a proverb by Pandarus, first to Troilus: 'A fool may ek a wis-man ofte gide' (I, 630), and then to Criseyde (using the potent verb): 'For wyse ben by foles harm *chastised*' (III, 329). The same idea is stated elsewhere by the Wife of Bath:

> *'Whoso that nyl be war by othere men,*
> *By hym shul othere men corrected be.'*
> (D, 180–1)

The lesson of the *Troilus* is related to the theme of exemplification, and it is Chaucer's technique, using the affective mode of late medieval meditative 'realism', to invite the reader first to identify with the example, and then, gradually, to disengage from it – not by moralistic condemnation, but through a process of perfected understanding based upon self-examination. I have called it, earlier, a 'trap' for the young at heart,[14] and it well may be so for that category of readers who, as the Wife says, 'wolde nat of hym corrected be' (D, 661); yet I think quite normally it belongs to the same technique of persuading the audience to grasp with the affections what they already assent to with the mind, as displayed in other late-fourteenth-and fifteenth-century forms, such as Franciscan lyrics and sermons, the drama of the York Realist, the *Confessio Amantis*, and the works of the Pearl Poet.

The seal of that technique, and the sign of the process of disengagement, come in the final, and most formal, call for correction, at the end of the poem as Chaucer directs his work to his friends. In its solemnity, it would seem to accord with the formula expressed by the Parson: 'this meditacioun / I putte it ay under correccioun / Of clerkes' (˘55–7); and suggests a height and a depth of concern that extend well beyond that earlier more fashionable and more playful appeal to lovers. The distance between these two appeals is a measure of the development of the lesson of the poem; which lesson I shall now proceed to summarize.

II

Bringing instruction into the world of romance raises the problem of diversion, in its several senses, and persuasion; and with these, the overall problem of tone. The poet who wishes to play the role of servant to the servants of Love does not have the option of prophecy or denunciation. Hence, he becomes an amiable ironist. He adopts the protective, affirmative diction of courtliness. He provides a mirror of polite society which seems to reflect its manners accurately, and he offers to tell a love story. But his story has an argument, which is to say, a thematic shape. It offers a lesson in the pursuit of happiness. And somewhere – at the start, in the middle, at the end – one begins to see that the narrator intends that the pursuit be evaluated critically.

At first, the story follows the archetype of the Rose, and the lovers happily adorn themselves with concepts which enhance their attractiveness. Troilus is gentle and true, Criseyde is true and honorable, and Pandarus is an honorable and gentle friend. At the same time, Troilus resigns his lordship, Criseyde declares she is not 'religious', and Pandarus ushers them onto the Wheel of Fortune. When the lovers are united, Troilus claims to have discovered that passion is charity. But what they fail to see, but Chaucer allows his audience to see more and more clearly, is that they have taken their sexual harmony either too seriously or not seriously enough. That is, in so thoroughly identifying it with the highest good, they have not prepared themselves to cope with the fortunes of the world and the rest of their life beyond the bed. If they had treated it as a very attractive game, perhaps the most attractive they had ever played, they would be less seriously trapped later on (but of course, we should not be so seriously interested in them, either). On the other hand, what they discover in the universe of each other's arms does not lead them anywhere except back to, and back to, bed. Their love, in terms of the *Roman de la Rose*, of Dante, or of Boethius, has not *taught* them enough.

Their chastisement has to be resumed after Book III, when the outer world breaks into their private affair. As their suffering increases, so does the anguish of their questioning. Criseyde draws one kind of conclusion, which seems to underscore the theme of mutability which our modern critics so favor:

> '*O brotel wele of mannes joie unstable!*
> *With what wight so thow be, or how thow pleye,*
> *Either he woot that thow, joie, art muable,*
> *Or woot it nought; it mot ben oon of tweye.*
> *Now if he woot it nought, how may he seye*
> *That he hath verray joie and selynesse,*
> *That is of ignoraunce ay in derknesse?*'
>
> (III, 820–6)

But what does she do with this undoubted piece of truth? She does nothing. It has only been part of her extravagant response to Pandarus's report of Troilus's jealousy, and a move in the continued game of defense she must play. But her assumption, finally, is that she is helpless – to stay happy, to be left alone, to survive in Troy independently. Her 'philosophy' never leads to any state except passivity. And, in even larger, longer, and louder terms, it is the same lesson which Troilus thinks his suffering confirms. No matter what he does, it has been his 'destiny' to love, and yet 'Fortune' is his foe.

Almost all readers suffer with Troilus's suffering, not merely because it is so prolixly lyrical, but mostly because it does not seem able to get him anywhere. If in Book III he is able to move with purpose, it is only after Pandarus has virtually carried him into Criseyde's presence, undressed him, and put him to bed. Failure to act does not qualify one, in most cases, to be a very interesting hero or heroine – which may explain part of the appeal Pandarus's constant 'bisynesse has for many.

Of course, in so far as the work is lyrical, it is content, as it assumes

31

we will be, to stand still and contemplate itself. Nevertheless, the *Troilus* is not a series of tableaux of songs and complaints. If it does not have the full range of physical action we expect from an epic or chivalric romance, it does have a movement and development within the world of thought and speech. This is to say, that the lyrics not only express states of mind but also ask questions. The questions relate to philosophical themes, even if the characters do not always recognize their implications; so that the 'problem' of action has a history in the poem which has even more interest than action itself. The drama is in the movements of the mind, which fact can remind us how close the lesson of the poem is to the great allegories in whose tradition it rests.

With Troilus and Criseyde, then, we are concerned with their freedom – freedom to love, freedom to be and remain their 'truest' selves, and freedom to act – and this leads us to examine the processes by which they recognize possibilities, make decisions, and determine their fate. Those who can act wisely are prudent (prudence was the applied, or active, form of wisdom). Those who refuse to act, or claim they are forced into inaction, have chosen folly. If Troilus is shown to be intelligent, it is so we may understand his folly; if he is shown to be noble, it is so we may grieve to see how he has wasted himself; and if he is shown to be supremely in love, it is so we may see how he has become enslaved rather than liberated by his passion. The greatest fallacy of the criticism I have been describing is to assume that Troilus had no alternatives, or could not discover what they were. In making him a representative of all humanity, they inevitably demean Chaucer's medieval humanism, which was based upon an uncomplicated belief in the freedom of the will and the splendor of reason.

III

I have chosen an example for this essay which will illustrate Troilus's unavailing self-chastisement, and which occurs late enough in the poem to accord with the readers' need to realize with greater objectivity the plight to which the characters have brought themselves. It is the extended soliloquy on free will in Book IV, an amplified counterpart to Criseyde's definition (III, 834) of the impossibility of happiness.

Pandarus has persuaded Criseyde to offer Troilus 'som wisdom' (IV, 928) to 'shapeth how destourbe youre goynge' (934), after the news of her exchange has been announced, and he goes off to find Troilus and lead him to her. He discovers him in a temple all alone, praying to the gods, and arguing his hopeless case. Chaucer gives Troilus 121 lines to pursue the theme, 'For al that comth, comth by necessitee: / Thus to ben lorn, it is my destinee' (IV, 958–9).

In his *The Textual Tradition of Chaucer's Troilus*, Robert Kilburn Root argues that the soliloquy was 'an afterthought', and that at one point, when Chaucer must have been busy with several important revisions, a scribe had left a blank space for the stanzas, with the note, 'her faileth thyng y' / is nat yt made'. There is no counterpart in Boccaccio's *Filostrato*. In the notes to his edition of the poem, Root has printed the relevant parallels to the soliloquy which are found in the *Boece*, V, pr 3, concerning the denial of free will. The logic of his argument with himself was summarized by Howard Rollin Patch and Walter Clyde Curry, and the passage has more recently been paraphrased by Ida Gordon in *The Double Sorrow of Troilus*.[15] There is no doubt that Chaucer has put into Troilus's mouth a rigidly necessitarian point of view, which, in Boethius's work, Lady Philosophy immediately goes on to refute. It is another example of the ironic application of philosophy to the romance, of – in Gordon's words – 'using Boethian arguments, recognizably but speciously, to reach a conclusion different from that to which those arguments led ultimately in the *Consolation*' (p. 46).

The reasoning, which is to say, the contents or the 'sentence', of the soliloquy has been sufficiently analyzed by these scholars to show that it relates to the theme of helplessness. Troilus cannot get around the conclusion that if 'God seth al biforn' (974), if follows that 'we han no fre chois' (980). He knows that some 'grete clerkes' have argued the contrary, but 'I not whos opynyoun I may holde' (973). He has been brooding about the course of action he should take, and emotionally may be suffering still from the paralyzing shock of sitting silent in 'parlement' while everyone else disposed – unreasonably and unjustly, it was apparent – of Criseyde's fate, and of his in hers (IV, 141–217). Chaucer shows him 'disputyng with hymself in this matere' (1084), thus continuing the theme of scholastic debate which had begun when Troilus argued, point by point, against Pandarus's proposals for solving his problems, concluding then, 'O, where hastow ben hid so longe in muwe, / That kanst so wel and formaly arguwe?' (IV, 496–7).

33

In other words, Troilus's performance completes a process of mind carefully developed by Chaucer in at least four stages: in the first, Troilus reasoned to rationalize his feelings; in the second, as in his hymn to Love, to articulate his religious faith; in the third, against Pandarus's ignobility in proposing that he abandon Troy and the lovers' honor; and finally, here, he reasons against Reason itself. The addition emphasizes the symmetrical contrast between this episode of antiphilosophy at the end of his wits, and the earlier episode of parodic philosophy when Pandarus offered his wit in the service of the 'ende' of passion. And now, all passion spent, Troilus declares, in effect, his intellectual bankruptcy.

The soliloquy is undistinguished verse but effective poetry. It is confusing, clotted, harsh, dry, contradictory, and involuted. Its rhythms tend towards doggerel or stretches of prose. It is ugly to hear. But it is as accurate a picture of Troilus's mind as Antigone's song was a mirror of the courtly mood. I think it is not difficult to argue that Chaucer can be seen here, not thriftily inserting a passage of straightforward philosophy he had recently been translating (the Boethian balades testify that he could versify grand ideas gracefully), but rather providing another excellent example of 'the forme of speche' which is emotionally and thematically appropriate.

Troilus is the proverbial ass, caught between the bale of hay and a bucket of oats. He oscillates. Here is one of my favorite examples:

> *'I mene as though I laboured me in this,*
> *To enqueren which thyng cause of which thyng be:*
> *As wheither that the prescience of god is*
> *The certeyn cause of the necessite*
> *Of thynges that to comen ben, parde;*
> *Or if necessite of thyng comynge*
> *Be cause certeyn of the purveyinge.'*
>
> (1009–15)

'Which causes which? Does God's foreknowledge make things necessarily happen so; or do things which happen necessarily cause God's foreknowledge?' Not only is it difficult to imagine that many could find such a question interesting, the stanza also makes it almost impossible to understand what is being asked. The Boethian original is hard enough: '(*thilke answere procedith ryght as though men travaileden or weren besy*) to enqueren the whiche thing is cause of the whiche thing, as whethir the prescience is cause of the necessite of thinges to comen, or elles that the necessite of thinges to comen is cause of the

34

purveaunce' (V, pr 3). This stanza from the *Troilus* is the closest Chaucer comes, in all his poetic translations, to making the shift no more than from unrhymed to rhymed prose, and from less to greater obscurity.

Shortly after this gyration, Troilus cites the example of one who sees a man sitting in a seat. What happens to the verse now is extraordinary:

> 'For if ther sitte a man yond on a see,
> Than by necessite bihoveth it
> That, certes, thyn opynyoun sooth be,
> That wenest or conjectest that he sit.
> And further over now ayeynward yit,
> Lo, right so is it of the part contrarie,
> As thus – nowe herkne, for I wol nat tarie:
>
> 'I sey, that if the opynyoun of the
> Be soth, for that he sitte, than sey I this,
> That he mot siten by necessite;
> And thus necessite in eyther is.'
>
> (1023–33)

Suddenly, there is a 'thou', and the man disputing with himself divides in two before our eyes. His muttering becomes more vehement, he imagines an adversary: 'nowe herkne, for I wol nat tarie'. Of line 1027, 'And further over now ayeynward yit', Root observes severely, if accurately, in his edition: '[it] is probably the least poetical line that Chaucer ever wrote' (p. 519).

Troilus has been wading in water that is too deep for him, a situation that Chaucer has always been inclined to treat with some humor, whether in the complaints of Palamon and Arcite in the *Knight's Tale*, the anguish of Dorigen on the rocks in the *Franklin's Tale*, or the sophisticated burlesque of *de casibus* metaphysics in the *Nun's Priest's Tale*. And so we see him, as we hear him, demonstrating his 'despeir' (IV, 954). The basic point of the soliloquy Chaucer gives him concerns his will, not just his emotions. Chaucer shows him choosing not to choose. Paradoxically, the passivity that so marks him subsequently is dramatized here as a condition actively entered into. And one can understand why Chaucer would come back to this crucial point in the poem, to amplify and develop it further. For it is through this final condition of despair, not the loss or the faithlessness of Criseyde, that the work becomes a tragedy.

IV

Such a conclusion is one the audience can come to more easily than the characters, particularly if Chaucer's first call to 'correccioun' has been heeded. For observe now, in retrospect, what sense those words can have for encountering the poem: 'for myne wordes . . . / I speke hem alle under correccioun / Of yow that felyng han in loves art.' Chaucer had continued:

> And putte it al in youre discrecioun
> To encresse or maken dymynucioun
> Of my langage, and that I yow biseche.
>
> (III, 1334–6)

'To encresse or maken dymynucioun' of Chaucer's language is not just to add to, or take away from, its superficial meaning. It is to join Chaucer in his grave, ironic game. It is not to read the poem exclusively as abstract philosophy or fashionable romance, but as a little bit of both, 'bitwixen ernest and game'. It is to understand its 'chastisement' as one we can both enjoy and contemplate.

The call for 'correccioun' is an appeal for validation, that the poem be truly understood. It is related to the other concern expressed at the end of the poem, 'so prey I God that non myswrite the, / Ne the mysmetre for defaute of tonge' (V, 1795–6) – and those lines lead to the sweeping prayer which follows:

> And red wherso thow be, or elles songe,
> That thow be understonde, God I biseche.
>
> (1797–8)

The call for correction is an appeal to be understood with the proper application.[16] And now we may examine that call at the end of the poem, which, in the light of the development of the lesson of chastisement and correction, rings completely true:

> O moral Gower, this book I directe
> To the and to the, philosophical Strode,
> To vouchen sauf, ther nede is, to correcte,
> Of your benignites and zeles goode.
>
> (V, 1856–9)

It is part of the maker's final ritual of validation. He emerges, putting off all his masks, discharging all his roles: he finishes as the lovers' humble servant, as the friend of ladies, as the reporter of

36

history, as the imitator of ancients, as the singer of divinity. Now he takes one more step forward and gives his own address, by citing the two friends who are most relevant to what the poem has done and means, and whose own authority can validate, or 'correct', what he has accomplished. There is now no reference to Lollius, no more mock apologies, no stylistic shape-shifting. Like his Parson, Chaucer will 'take but the sentence' (9, 58) now that he has left his fable behind.

This particular appeal to these particular friends is conclusive evidence that Chaucer means us to take more meaning than sad mutability from the conclusion of his poem. The epithets and the names, 'moral Gower' and 'philosophical Strode', are equally important. The words for this stanza, the seal of his personal speaking, are as carefully chosen and as thematically relevant as anywhere else.

That both men were long-time associates and good friends of Chaucer is likely, and has been carefully, if not conclusively, documented by John H. Fisher.[17] The *Life Records* of Chaucer show some documentation for their mutual association through the legal system, as in granting power of attorney, or standing as mainpernor.[18] All that survives of Strode's work are treatises and texts on logic,[19] with no acknowledgment by him of Chaucer – whereas Gower places Chaucer's name in a prominent position in the earlier version of his ending of the *Confessio Amantis*.[20] Strode would have been one of the more prominent names Chaucer could have invoked; he was a scholar and a public servant.[21] He had been a fellow of Merton College in 1359–60, and was the Common Serjeant or Pleader (i.e. the public prosecutor) of the City of London, 1373–82, and then the Standing Counsel until his death in 1387. He engaged in some amicable controversy with John Wyclif, after his controversial *De Civili Dominio* was published c.1377, but only Wyclif's replies have survived.[22] As to why Chaucer should appeal to him for correction, I can suppose two reasons: that Strode's interest in 'philosophy' corresponded to its prominence in the *Troilus*; and that his 'style' in learning accorded with Chaucer's strategy in arranging the chastisement of the poem.

As to the philosophy of Strode, there exist the treatises on logic, which gained him an international reputation.[23] Even more to the point are his *argumenta* addressed to Wyclif, for these show him to be pressing Wyclif on the more severe aspects of his theology of predestination. We cannot tell what reasoning Strode followed, but it is fascinating to see much the same vocabulary involved in some of

37

Wyclif's replies as appears in Troilus's soliloquy, including the startling *omnia que evenient de neccessitate evenient* ('all things that happen happen by necessity').[24] Tatlock summarizes his position: 'Ralph Strode as a theologian seems to have been a thorough conservative, who fought Wyclif's doctrine of predestination as inconsistent with man's free will', but I think he misses the point when he suggests that 'Strode would have been an uncompromising critic' of Chaucer's poem ('The Epilog', p. 145, n. 2). Chaucer is to Troilus-the-character on the subject of free will as Strode is to Wyclif. The dedication to Strode confirms the poem's serious and elaborate development of 'philosophical' themes.

Furthermore, it is particularly the conservative, that is to say, the moderate, aspects of Strode, as opposed to the extremist, or reformist, aspects of Wyclif, which suggest he could appreciate the artistic development of those themes. The *argumenta* addressed to Wyclif stress the danger of precipitous reform, and recommend the priority of the peace of the church and the worship of God. Wyclif honors these objections. As Herbert B. Workman observes, 'he would agree that reformation "should not be sudden but carried out with prudence and step by step". As Wyclif makes no further reference . . . to his former friend in any of his writings, it is probable that the breach between the two became as complete as that between Erasmus and Luther.'[25] I find it appropriate to think of this notable man – whom the irascible Wyclif treated with respect and affection – as an Erasmus, for Erasmian qualities of tolerance and temperance shine through the 'chastisement' of the *Troilus* – where, too, reformation, or the access to wisdom, cannot 'be sudden but [must be] carried out with prudence and step by step'.

Fisher makes an important distinction between 'philosophical' and 'moral' as terms, which further elucidates Chaucer's pairing his two friends in the final directive: 'To Chaucer "philosophical" denoted speculative and intellectual excellence. . . . Strode would have been expected to be interested in the astronomical and astrological lore . . . [and] would have appreciated the Boethian treatments of necessity and free will, false felicity, fortune and destiny' (pp. 225–6). We may conclude, quite in opposition to Tatlock's opinion, that Strode would have confirmed the 'trouthe' of Chaucer's learning concerning the astrological and psychological forces in the poem, the subtlety in treating the applications and misapplications of logic, and the skill in dramatizing the debate between destiny and free will – all in an urbane, non-denunciatory, and friendly fashion.

The appeal to 'philosophical Strode', then, is an appeal on grounds of wisdom, of intellectual sophistication and completeness. It is perfectly in accord with those qualities of the poet which his contemporary, Thomas Usk, praised so highly. In Usk's *The Testament of Love* (c.1387), the persona called Love, who turns out to be another Lady Philosophy distributing Boethian doctrine, refers to Chaucer as 'myne owne trewe servaunt, the noble philosophical poete in Englissh', and refers a question of the 'prescience of god and free arbitrement' to 'a tretis that he made of my servant Troilus' – where the matter was 'touched, and at the ful this question assoyled'. She concludes, 'in witte and in good reson of sentence he passeth al other makers. In the boke of Troilus, the answere to thy question mayst thou lerne.'[26]

On the other hand, to turn also to 'moral Gower' was to balance the appeal, for this meant stressing the active virtue of prudence, along with the speculative one of wisdom. As Fisher writes, '*philosophia moralis* had designated the branch of philosophy dealing with the principles of human conduct' and *virtus moralis* meant 'excellence of character as distinguished from excellence of intellect' (p. 226). He cites Venus's address to Gower at the end of the *Confessio*:

> '*And tarie thou mi Court nomore,*
> *Bot go ther vertu moral duelleth,*
> *Wher ben thi bokes, as men telleth,*
> *Whiche of long time thou hast write.*'
> (VIII, 2924–7)

He concludes: 'Chaucer was as conscious of the moral dimension of the *Troilus* as he was of its learning, and . . . he submitted its moral philosophy to the correction of John Gower' (p. 227). Gower's *Confessio* makes a fitting comparison with the *Troilus* because of its explicit link to Chaucer and its search for a reconciliation between love and morality. Although I cannot do honor to its particular solution as a chastisement set 'bitwixen ernest and game' – or, as Gower describes it, a 'middel weie . . . somwhat of lust, somwhat of lore' (Prologus, 17, 19) – because the tone is not consistently ironic, nor the persona of Genius, the Lover's preceptor, consistently portrayed; and although its literary impression seems to me a blurred melting together of poeticisms and pedantry, still the lesson of the work is not confused in conception, even if sometimes contradictory in execution. And that lesson makes it very clear that one can love virtuously, as a human, on earth, before death.[27]

Gower's Genius, after discussing the nature of *gentilesse*, adds:

> 'And overthis, mi Sone, also
> After the vertu moral eke
> To speke of love if I schal seke,
> Among the holi bokes wise
> I finde write in such a wise,
> "Who loveth noght is hier as ded";
> For love above alle othre is hed,
> Which hath the vertus forto lede,
> Of al that unto mannes dede
> Belongeth.'
>
> (IV, 2320–9)

The gloss to this passage – 'Nota de amore caritatis' – reminds us how much it resembles Raison's claim, in the Romance of the Rose, that she knows an appropriate love, not a hate, which the Lover could use. Charity is the love described by 'the holi bokes wise'. And indeed, Genius will admonish the Lover:

> My Sone, and if thou have be so,
> Yit is it time to withdrawe,
> And set thin herte under that lawe,
> The which of reson is governed
> And noght of will.
>
> (VIII, 2132–6)

This counsel to withdraw is a call to active prudence.

The dichotomy between Reason and the Will is the same through the ages, as applicable to Troilus as to the 'yonge fresshe folkes' of medieval England. The Christian revelation of grace may have illuminated some things which had previously been dark, and added the theological to the cardinal virtues, but one should not conclude that Troilus and Criseyde could not have loved reasonably (in fact, Cicero used the word 'charity' to describe his conception of ideal friendship). The exemplar of 'trouthe', good Queen Alceste, although not a Christian, was a good wife and a true lover. Besides, Chaucer is not inviting his audience to play god (or Minos) and decide the fate of the souls of the Trojan population; he is directing them to 'withdrawe' to that position where they may fully understand the story as exemplary. And from that position, the contraries are not so much tensely opposed as manifestly placed in order.

Chaucer's final appeal for correction places him back in our world and reminds us of the full range of resources – from Strode's 'philosophy' to Gower's 'moralitee' – we have for correcting our own vision. For it is *choice* which is at the heart of Chaucer's lesson, as it is related to love, war, and destiny, and one's capacity to know, 'to see the ende', which determines the kind of choice one makes and its outcome, whether tragic, comic, or pathetic. It is the folly of Troilus's will which first moves and entertains us; it is, finally, our own world of knowing and choosing which Chaucer's art aims to affect. His closing, neither a true Epilogue nor a Palinode, is a finishing off, a bringing up of all the lights at the end of the lesson. The pagan world is firmly placed within the frame of the salvation-history a Christian audience would know. The gods are dismissed as figures, or phantoms, of speech. The 'pitee' of Cupid's church is turned into the affection of the narrator towards those 'in which that love upgroweth with your ages'. The deferential entertainer has been transformed into the friend of Strode and Gower. The language of the courtly world is continued, raised, and translated into the terms of his gracious appeal, with its polite verb, 'vouchen sauf', in 'vouchen sauf, ther nede is, to correcte', until it is speech of religious appeal, come home at last. First, there is the address to the 'yonge fresshe folkes, he or she', and now, here is his appeal to his friends' 'benignites and zeles goode' (1859).

'Benignite' is a word for goodness referring to one's spiritual graciousness. Chaucer used it at the start of the poem, in his bidding prayer to lovers asking them to pray

> *God, for his benignite,*
> *So graunte hem soone owt of this world to pace,*
> *That ben despeired out of Loves grace;*
>
> (I, 40–3)

and it was only under the apparent aegis of Cupid that he would ask for God's grace to be displayed in ending the lives of those in despair. It is also the word Chaucer used in praying Venus for inspiration, at the beginning of Book III (39), and was in Troilus's hymn, to 'Benigne Love, thow holy bond of thynges' (III, 1261). But now, as everything lifts into a final clarity of regard, his appeal is to the 'benignity' of his learned and moral friends – and also, to their 'zeles', a word which occurs here, and nowhere else, in Chaucer's work.

I take 'zeles' to mean 'fervent love', with Biblical and religious overtones.[28] The love humans can know does not stay behind, locked in the anguish of the world of Troy, nor need it be restricted to the

41

ascetic zone of the convent. It may be expressed by friends, by friends' learning, and by friends' 'correccioun'. And in the case of a poem about love, it may be found in the 'zeles' of a listening and reading audience who will give themselves as carefully to it as it was given to them.

Realism in *Troilus and Criseyde* and the *Roman de la Rose*

JAMES I. WIMSATT

In a recent essay I attempted to show that in *Troilus and Criseyde* there are three literary frames-of-reference which Chaucer builds up quite elaborately and then undercuts.[1] Through the devices, conventions, and commonplaces of Dantean epic, Machauvian romance, and Boethian demonstration he suggests alternately and sometimes simultaneously that the narrative of *Troilus* presents heroic love or ideal lovers, or that it amounts to an indictment or defence of Providence. He does not sustain these suggestions, however, thoroughly undermining them with irony. What he does sustain, after negating all such pretensions, is realism, which he builds up with circumstantial detail, unidealized incident, psychological interaction, and a love story that unfolds according to a common and natural pattern. This realism makes *Troilus* a new kind of literature; the claim of the older critics that it is the first modern novel makes a certain amount of sense.

To say that the realism of *Troilus* is new, though, is not to say that there was no background for it, that it developed *ex nihilo*. It has been noted that while Pallas Athene sprang full-grown, it was the brain of a god that gave her birth. Everything human is part of a continuum. This principle applies particularly to literature, as critics have asserted in various ways.[2] A literary theorist who makes the point in a way that I find particularly applicable to medieval literature and the question at hand is E. D. Hirsch, Jr. Hirsch speaks of the necessity, for both an author's creation and a reader's understanding, of 'preexisting type conceptions'.[3] From previous experience with literature a writer will conceive and a reader will infer what Hirsch calls the 'intrinsic genre' of a work. This intrinsic genre repeats, develops from, or combines the genre or genres of previous works.[4] Prior literature, then, provides a frame-of-reference in which a new work becomes comprehensible and interpretable.

Misconceptions about the applicable frame-of-reference can lead to wildly mistaken readings. *Troilus* and the *Roman de la Rose*, for instance, have both been misread as being of a kind with nineteenth-century romantic fiction, as if Lord Byron and Henri Murger's Bohemians were in their backgrounds. The literary contexts which go to form the intrinsic genre of a work must pre-exist it; they are often revealed by echoes and direct borrowings of antecedent writings. It is true that even heavy borrowings may lead the reader astray, as, for example, is the case with Chaucer's uses of Machaut in *Troilus* whose romantic implications he negates. *Troilus* is not essentially about a heaven for lovers. But more typically borrowings provide immediate clues to the applicable generic contexts. Thus, important aspects of the realism of *Troilus* reflect, and may be understood in the context of, fourteenth-century Italian narrative, this being predictable considering the importance of Boccaccio's *Filostrato* as a source.

The contribution of Italian stories to the realism of *Troilus*, though, while substantial, is liable to be overestimated. The elements of realism that I wish to deal with in this paper derive from two other medieval types, or genres, which also supply sources for *Troilus*, though less conspicuous ones than Boccaccio. These types, both of which develop from classical models, are the Arts of Love, or handbooks for lovers, and the Platonic cosmic fables. It is not strange that the two types likewise provide major sources for the *Roman de la Rose*, for it too, despite the allegorical method, has certain basic realism, comprising an analysis of a typical courtship that culminates in intercourse. In the light of Chaucer's familiarity with the *Roman*, it is especially informative to consider aspects of realism in the two works at the same time.

The family of cosmic fables originates with Plato's *Timaeus*, and it includes Cicero's *Dream of Scipio* as expounded by Macrobius, Martianus Capellas's *Marriage of Mercury and Philology*, Boethius's *Consolation of Philosophy*, and a number of later poems by the twelfth-century 'Chartrians': Bernard Silvestris's *Cosmographia*, Alan of Lille's *Anticlaudianus* and *De planctu naturae*, and John of Hanville's *Architrenius*. The Arts of Love have their inception in Ovid's *Ars amatoria* and *Remedia amoris*, along with the sketches of the *Amores*, and the genre flowers in the twelfth and thirteenth centuries with several translations and adaptations of Ovid, with the *De amore* of Andreas Capellanus, itself translated into French by Drouart la Vache, and – very important for our consideration – with the popular Latin story called *Pamphilus*, subtitled in manuscript *De amore*, whose French version is known as *Pamphile et Galathée*.[5]

Ovid's treatises on love were the prototypes of the medieval Art of Love genre, and when Guillaume de Lorris proclaims at the beginning of his work that it contains the whole 'Art d'Amors' (l. 38)[6] Ovid surely is evoked. The Roman's witty poems of the type, in part responsible for his exile, are decorated with mythological references and narratives, but their essence lies in the narrator's humorous, and quite practical, instructions for getting and keeping the lady of one's choice, or, alternatively, giving her up. In the *Ars amatoria* the advice is enlivened with realistic description of scenes at the circus, at banquets, and at the theatre. In the *Remedia amoris* the realism at times declines to crudity: 'Her gait is awkward? Take her for a walk. Her breast is all swelling paps? Let no bands conceal the fault. If her teeth are ugly tell her something to make her laugh. Are her eyes weak? Recount a tearful tale' (337–40).[7]

Guillaume de Lorris in no place is so vulgar; he is, after all, not presenting remedies. Yet it is this very *Remedia amoris* which suggested the portress of Guillaume's paradisal garden. 'Otia' – 'Oiseuse', 'Idleness' – says Ovid in the *Remedia*, 'makes you love; it guards what it has done; it is the cause and sustenance of the pleasant evil' (136–38). And Ovidian realism is pervasive in the *Roman*, both parts. Guillaume's God of Love, who lectures Amant after he has shot him, while more decorous than the narrator of the *Remedia*, is a notable purveyor of such realism. He gives Amant grooming tips – 'Brush your teeth', 'Comb your hair' – and he envisions vivid scenes of Amant's future experiences, as when he will haunt the lady's house at night, sighing through the keyhole. Substantial borrowings from the *Ars amatoria* for the god's lecture confirm a close filiation between Guillaume and Ovid in this part.[8] In turn Jean de Meun uses several hundred lines from the same work for the speeches of Ami and La Vieille. Another Art of Love, that of Andreas, supplies the definition of love enunciated by Jean's Raison (4377–84).[9] And Jean's description of the poem as a Mirror for Lovers (10651) indicates that he shares Guillaume's conception of the work. 'Art d'Amors' and 'Mirouer aus amoureus' equally characterize a manual of instruction on the subject of love, thus equally claim a part in the genre.

A line of influence that attaches the story of the *Roman* integrally to the Art of Love family is that which comes to it through the twelfth-century Latin *Pamphilus*. *Pamphilus* features both Ovidian lessons about love and the application of these lessons in a narrative. Guillaume's probable verbal borrowings from the work are modest in extent, and Jean evidently makes none, but, as Ernest Langlois has shown, in other ways the French narrative is based importantly on the Latin poem:

> [The two works] have the same object: to show the application of the theories presented in the Arts of Love by putting on stage characters who act in conformity with the rules taught in these treatises . . . In [*Pamphilus*] the young man, wounded to the heart, addresses himself to Venus and asks how he can gain the love of her who alone can cure him, and the goddess teaches him ways to seduce the young lady; in [the *Roman*] it is the God of Love who dictates his precepts to the young man, equally struck to the heart, and who teaches him how he can find a remedy for his wound. Pamphilus, in order to arrive more surely at his goal, approaches an old woman who has the confidence of the parents of Galathea and who misuses it to serve the loves of the two young people. When Guillaume de Lorris interrupts his romance, he has just introduced the character of La Vieille, to whom Jalousie, that is, the parents, have confided the guard over Bel Acueil. Now it is evident that the duenna was to play in the story a role analogous to that she filled in the Latin poem. . . . Pamphilus, Galathea, the old woman, and the goddess of Love are the sole actors in the Latin poem. Guillaume de Lorris added others . . . but these new parts of Jalousie, Male-Bouche, Honte, Peur, and even that of Ami are already indicated in *Pamphilus*.[10]

There may be some overstatement of the indebtedness here, but Langlois adduces substantial textual support for his assertions.[11] All in all, it seems that *Pamphilus* is an essential influence on the narrative of Guillaume de Lorris, and furthermore provides a basis for several speakers and actors whom Jean de Meun develops at length.

Pamphilus continued to be popular through the fourteenth century. The central love story of Juan Ruiz's famous *Libro de Buen Amor* (c.1330) is drawn directly from it. And it seems probable, as Thomas J. Garbáty maintains, that in *Troilus and Criseyde* Chaucer made use of both the Latin and Spanish poems.[12] Garbáty cites extensive, impressive parallels between the first three books of *Troilus* and the two works. Many of these involve the character of Pandarus, who more integrally than Boccaccio's Pandaro participates in the Art of Love genre, particularly in the literary tradition of the bawd that begins with Ovid's Dipsas[13] and continues with the Anus of *Pamphilus*, La Vieille of the *Roman*, and Convent-Trotter (Trotaconventos) of the *Libro de Buen Amor*. Pandarus, like Boccaccio's go-between, is anxious to differentiate himself from the bawd, but the parallels between him and the Anus of *Pamphilus* are impressive: both Pandarus and the Anus are presented as senior advisers in love, experienced in the old dance; both claim a special relationship with the beloved that will help ease the lover's problems; both hurry to the lady, using similar strategy to whet her curiosity and desire – flattering her, praising him to her, and impressing on her the desirability of loving before age takes its toll. The similarities multiply, the most striking coming in the trickery the go-betweens use in bringing about the union of the lovers. Garbáty summarizes:

> Finally the intermediaries decide on a plan. They invite the ladies to their homes to eat, and assure them that they will be safe from gossip and rumor. In the meantime, after a speech on destiny to the lover, in which she says that God alone can foretell the future, the Anus causes Pamphilus to swoon, arousing his jealousy by lying to him about a rival in love; Pandarus parallels this action when he mentions to Criseyde the 'jealousy' of Troilus for Horaste. In preparation for the consummation, the go-between tells the lover to 'be a man'. As the lady is eating at the house of the intermediary, they hear a wind and the lover comes in abruptly. The go-between breaks out in sentimental, sympathetic tears for the lovers and quickly leaves them alone. The men order the women to yield. . . . With the morning, the go-between returns and innocently asks what has happened, how the night was passed? The Anus and Pandarus are immediately and roundly accused of trickery and treachery by the women.[14]

Garbáty enumerates a number of further parallels between *Troilus* and the *Libro de Buen Amor*, those between the two intermediaries again being prominent. If Pandarus is not directly drawn from the bawds in these works, he must be modelled in substantial ways on close literary relatives of them.

The character of Pandarus is the main link between Chaucer's poem and the Art of Love Genre. Like the bawds of *Pamphilus* and

Juan Ruiz he helps to put into action the practical precepts of Amor. Equally important, as a colorful, witty, and unidealistic preceptor of Love, he is allied to the narrator of Ovid's treatises, to Venus in *Pamphilus*, to the God of Love and Ami in the *Roman de la Rose*, as well as to the various old crones who speak from long experience in the works. Frequent echoes of Ovid and the *Roman* in the extensive counselling of Pandarus and his imprecations of the lovers substantiate the connection.[15]

As a result of their kinship with the Arts of Love, the narratives of both the *Roman* and *Troilus* maintain a close connection with the world of fact and of practical action. While love romances like those of Machaut and Froissart customarily present scenes that occur only in the minds of lovers and in other romances, the Arts posit realistic activity tending toward unequivocal worldly goals. The bawds, bedrooms, and billets-doux of these works are common and convenient facilitators of mundane carnal union. These impart to the action circumstantial verisimilitude. At the same time, despite the clear filiations, it is no doubt manifest to all readers that it will not do to pass off either of these works as in their essence simply Arts of Love. There is more to the realism of the *Roman* and of *Troilus* than the cynical practicality of such works. Though it is true that the Arts of Love often are characterized by delicate literary decoration and by a certain courtliness in the manners represented, their assumptions in many ways are on a level with the fabliaux. The love affairs in *Troilus* and the *Roman* are more humane. Their realism is more searching and profound, made so in part by their participation in the frame-of-reference of the cosmic allegories.

Major members of the family of cosmic allegories, as I have said, are the Platonic fables of Macrobius, Martianus Capella, and Boethius, and the twelfth-century Chartrian epics of Bernard Silvestris and Alan of Lille.[16] In the second part of the *Roman* Jean de Meun imitates or translates more than five thousand lines of Alan's *De planctu naturae*, makes Alan's Nature and Genius central characters in his allegory, and draws his description of Fortune's home from Alan's *Anticlaudianus*.[17] These direct borrowings clearly signal the alliance of Jean's work with the cosmic allegories. That this alliance, even as with the Arts of Love, develops out of his predecessor Guillaume's use and reflection of these allegories is not so manifest, or at least has not been evident to critics.[18] *Troilus and Criseyde* likewise has affiliations with the allegories that have not been accurately perceived.

The cosmic allegories are particularly concerned with displaying a

Platonic scheme which explains the operation of the universe. In the Chartrian development of these works there is an increasing concern with the earthly aspects of creation, notably with human reproduction. As a result, it was just a step from Alan of Lille's allegories, wherein Nature's governance of procreation is a large concern, to representation of archetypal sexual experience. Guillaume de Lorris and Jean de Meun took this step and produced the *Roman de la Rose*. It was a little longer step to the investing of archetypal sexual narrative with a local habitation. Chaucer in *Troilus and Criseyde* took that step. The actions in the *Roman* and *Troilus* are in the first place motivated by the power of cosmic forces. Even though the affairs in both poems are abetted by controllable human allies – Ovidian commentators and manipulators like Pandarus and Ami – the more powerful propellant is the force of Nature which is virtually uncontrollable. Consequently, while in moral terms the lovers of these stories are intemperate in their treatment of each other, they do not manifest the single-minded selfishness which characterizes Ovidian lovers. Blind stimuli rather than calculating cupidity supply the main motivation. Such stimuli invest the actions and reactions of the characters with a spontaneity and fidelity to common human behavior which is deeply realistic.

In order to explicate the part the Platonic fables play in the *Roman* and *Troilus*, it will be helpful to refer to the works of Bernard Silvestris and Alan of Lille, to Chaucer's *Parliament of Fowls*, which is a relatively unadulterated offspring of the Chartrian works, and to the most ambitious imitation of the *Roman de la Rose*, the *Échecs amoureux*, whose poet reveals a particular consciousness of Guillaume's debt to the Chartrian works.

The Garden of Deduit of the *Roman* originates in the cosmic allegories. Bernard Silvestris depicts a garden, Granusion, where Nature and Urania join Physis to create the microcosmos, man.[19] In this garden soul and body are united, planetary influences take effect on earthly objects, and Platonic exemplars are converted to individual shapes. It is in a broad sense a garden of generation, and Bernard identifies it with Eden,[20] appropriately so, since it was in Eden that God 'brought forth all manner of trees' (Genesis ii. 9), and created man and woman, and in which Adam assigned names to all 'the beasts of the earth' and 'the fowls of the air' (ii. 18). Clearly related to Bernard's Granusion, though not explicitly connected with Eden, is the garden of Nature presented in the *Anticlaudianus* of Alan of Lille.[21] Here procreation is the implicit concern. On an elevated plane in the center of the garden Nature's palace is erected, in which she paints the pictures by which she 'turns the shadows of things into things',[22] that is, makes worldly entities from exemplars. Despite the beauty of the garden, it is clearly post-lapsarian, for beside Nature's pictures of wisdom and strength appear images of vice and profligacy.

The process by which Nature perpetuates the human race is more elaborately presented in Alan's other major allegory, *De planctu naturae*. In this work Nature introduces herself as a deputy of God, 'a coiner for stamping the order of things'.[23] Venus is her sub-vicar, she says, whom she has appointed 'in order that she, under my judgment and guidance, and with the assisting activity of her husband Hymen and her son Cupid, by laboring at the various formation of the living things of earth, and regularly applying their productive hammers to their anvils, might weave together the line of the human race in unwearied continuation'.[24]

When in *De planctu* Nature names Cupid, the narrator interrupts and prevails on her to speak more broadly of Venus's son. Nature begins with a spate of oxymorons: 'Love is peace joined with hatred . . . healthy sickness . . . sweet evil . . . living death', and so on. She asserts the power which Cupid has over all men, and concludes that the only way to escape his dominion is to flee him.[25] Later Nature presents a variant allegorical explanation of the contradictory aspects of sexual love. She explains that Venus and her proper husband Hymen gave birth to Cupid, while as a result of adultery with a character called Antigamus (Anti-marriage) Venus also brought forth Jocus (Mirth), who contrasts sharply with his brother. Whereas Cupid is cultured and courteous, Jocus is gross and brutal. Jocus pitches his tent in the desert – that is, is sterile[26] – while Cupid makes his home in the wooded valley. Cupid wounds with golden spears, but Jocus with iron javelins.[27]

A good analogue to the dual symbolism of the sons of Venus in the *De planctu* is presented by the dual inscription at the garden entrance in Chaucer's *Parliament of Fowls*, one side promising everlasting 'grene and lusty May' (130), the other that 'nevere tre shal fruyt ne leves bere' (137). The garden of the *Parliament* is consistent with the inscription; Nature presides, with both procreative and sterile love having their places, the former in the 'launde' where the assembly of birds takes place and the latter in the temple of Venus. In the *Parliament* Chaucer acknowledges his debt to Alan by name. At the same time for the garden description he draws on the *Roman de la Rose*,[28] signalling indirectly what direct inspection verifies, that Guillaume's *locus amoenus* too is related to the gardens of the Chartrian poets.

That Guillaume's dreamer, like Chaucer's in the *Parliament*, is to enter on a journey into a Platonic region is indicated by references to Macrobius and the Dream of Scipio at the beginning of the work.[29] The lengthy opening of the *Échecs amoureux*, all of which poem is a patent imitation of the *Roman*, similarly and much more elaborately invokes the frame-of-reference of the cosmic allegories.[30] In the *Échecs*, furthermore, the poet explicitly attributes Guillaume's garden to the illegitimate son of Venus.[31] The attribution both connects the garden of the *Roman* with Alan's allegory and identifies it as a debased garden of generation.[32] There are several additional connections of Guillaume's poem with the allegories. The robe of Guillaume's God of Love, made to resemble the robe of Alan's Nature, reveals him as an agent of Nature.[33] Also Guillaume's bright-eyed Raison who descends to Amant is identified unmistakably with Boethius's Lady Philosophy[34] and thereby with the numerous Wisdom figures of the cosmic fables, including Martianus's Philology, Bernard's Nous and her subsidiary goddesses, and several of Alan's most important personifications.[35] And, most significant, when Venus uses her torch to induce Bel Acueil to grant a kiss to Amant (3473–76), then the function of Venus as an elemental procreative urge, which is stimulated by physical propinquity, seems carefully delineated. In both attribute and function she is like the planetary Venus of Bernard Silvestris. The 'distinguishing ornament' of Venus, says Bernard in *Cosmographia*, is a torch; he notes the astrologers' dictum that 'whatever incites the human longing for pleasure becomes vehement through the influence of Venus's star'.[36]

Taking into account the sum of these echoes of the cosmic allegories in Guillaume's part, it is obvious that when Jean de Meun depicts Venus and Raison in accordance with the tradition of cosmic allegory, and introduces Nature and Genius as central figures, he is developing the poem in line with Guillaume's representation, even as he was following Guillaume's Art of Love in constructing a Mirror for Lovers.

Though with their abstract and often florid presentations the Platonic works seem anything but realistic, in using these narratives the poets of the *Roman* were concerned with typical affairs of human life, the sphere of realism. Alan's characterization of Venus and her husbands and children is designed to show and rationalize the practices of sexual love in the world. Guillaume de Lorris's aim in the Roman accords with this purpose and his representation carries Alan's a degree closer to the world of fact. The image of Love's dance which Guillaume employs is an apt one, for his narrative shows an archetypal mating dance carried on under the aegis of Idleness and Mirth. Guillaume imports into the cosmic garden a particular man in love with a particular woman. He assures us that the dream has historical veracity: 'There is nothing which did not happen just as the dream tells it' (28–30). Yet when the dreamer enters the garden he takes on the character of the generic Amant, and his specific love affair assumes archetypal significance. The narrator, then, is both the unique Guillaume and the representative Amant. His story thereby accords with a fundamental requirement of literary realism; it is a commonplace of criticism that successful realism presents actions that are in some fashion at the same time general and specific.[37]

The pattern of action, so far as Guillaume de Lorris carries it, embodies a familiar and predictable human paradigm. It begins with the lover's enamourment and his first approach to the lady, which she receives in friendly fashion; his ensuing aggression, however, excites her fear and 'danger'. His gentle coaxing soothes her and gains a kiss, but then follow quickly the neighbors' gossip, the family's disapproval, her rebuff of him, his anguish and recourse to reason for comfort, and the failure of reason. In Venus's inciting the lady to grant a kiss, the power of Nature is explicitly depicted, but we must feel in addition that the whole of this story proceeds archetypally, and that it is imperatives of the divine mind, passed down into the world by Nature through Venus, which ultimately impel all the action. These imperatives in their operation on human kind become in large part misdirected as a result of the adultery of Venus – that is to say, as a result of the Fall – but they still summon king and churl, along with all living things, to Love's dance. Thus, though Ovidian art and artifice account for much of the discussion and even of the action in the *Roman*, Nature is the main force impelling the lovers' behavior.

The case is much the same with *Troilus and Criseyde*, as the narrator indicates explicitly early in the story:

> For evere it was, and evere it shal byfalle,
> That Love is he that alle thing may bynde,
> For may no man fordon the lawe of kynde.
> (I, 236–8)

The artifice of Pandarus facilitates the union of Troilus and his lady, and the story gains immeasurable interest as a result of his participation. But the magnet that inexorably pulls the lovers together is the 'lawe of kynde', as is confirmed by the powerful emotions which accompany the predictable stages in their affair. As with the *Roman de la Rose*, the story of these lovers is archetypal, and it too is associated with the cosmic allegories, though the connection is by no means so broadly based as with the *Roman*. It is most apparent in Book III, and in the Epilogue that closes the poem. Book III, preponderantly taken up with the raptures of love, is indeed the book of Venus. Its boundaries are like temporal walls enclosing a paradise of Love, for the narrative of the poem is so divided that the lover's first physical contact occurs at the opening of the book, and within the book are contained the consummation and *all* the time of their content. Before Book III come the arduous preliminaries; immediately following the fateful exchange is arranged. But within its compass little seems to dispute that celestial Venus is directly manifesting her influence in the congress of the lovers. Of this both Troilus and the narrator are convinced.

The *Parliament of Fowls* has in common with Book III of *Troilus* that its overriding concern is with mating. In the *Parliament* just before relating his dream the narrator calls on planetary Venus and her torch:

> *Cytherea! thow blysful lady swete,*
> *That with thy fyrbrond dauntest whom the lest.*
> (113–4)

So too at the beginning of Book III the narrator invokes planetary Venus:

> *O blisful light, of which the bemes clere*
> *Adorneth al the thridde heven faire!*
> (1–2)

The impressive invocation (1–49), derived in part ultimately from Boethius and directly in the line of the cosmic allegories, deals with the operation of divine love in the universe, particularly as felt in the world by 'man, brid, best, fissh, herbe, and grene tree' (10). What the invocation says about cosmic love, and its association with planetary Venus, is accurate in terms of the philosophers' fables except that the perversion of sexual love by man is ignored. The narrator cites only the benign effects of the torch:

> *Algates hem that ye wol sette a-fyre,*
> *They dreden shame, and vices they resygne;*
> *Ye do hem corteys be, fresshe and benigne.*
> (24–6)

53

He forgets the rent in Nature's gown caused by man's fall. Following the narrator's lead, Troilus twice in the course of the book prayerfully addresses planetary Venus, the first time together with other beneficial planets (705, 712–35), and the second (1254–74) together with Hymen, whom Alan identifies as her legal husband, and with her son, 'Benigne Love, thow holy bond of thynges' (1261). And Troilus's final paean in Book III is addressed to

> *Love, that of erthe and se hath governance,*
> *Love, that his hestes hath in hevenes hye.*
> (1744–5)

Drawn directly from Boethius, this poem of praise forcefully sustains the cosmic context right to the end of the book.

As I have indicated, while these prayers in *Troilus* are very impressive, in context they are not entirely appropriate; they ignore the fact that the garden of love that Book III comprises belongs to Jocus. Planetary Venus's influence is perverted to mirthful love. Nevertheless, though the love presented is debased with all else about humanity after the Fall, it remains part of the universal order, as it does in the allegory of *De planctu* and the *Roman*. The power and beauty of the order, therefore, is manifested in the love of Troilus and Criseyde, whatever their rational errors and moral faults. It shows up especially in their emotional and physical transports. That they genuinely participate in the harmony of nature is emphasized and underlined by the images, closely following one another in the consummation scene, that repeatedly associate them with the flora and fauna of the natural world:

> *What myghte or may the sely larke seye,*
> *Whan that the sperhauk hath it in his foot?*
> (1191–2)

> *Right as an aspes leef she gan to quake.*
> (1200)

> *And as aboute a tree, with many a twiste,*
> *Bytrent and writh the swote wodebynde,*
> *Gan ech of hem in armes other wynde.*
> (1230–2)

> *And as the newe abaysed nyghtyngale,*
> *That stynteth first whan she bygynneth to synge*
>
> . . . .
>
> *Right so Criseyde.* . . .
>
> (1233–8)

Chaucer's presentation of this scene provides a powerful poetic image of instinctive sexual attraction which has essential realism. The spiritual level of romance that the lovers postulate is illusory, but there is a natural level of tender love that is genuine and true to life. Even in Book IV, when their ideal world has dissolved, the lovers can rejoice as, like 'briddes', they join in 'th'amourouse daunce' (IV, 1431–2). As in the *Roman de la Rose* the whole affair proceeds according to a natural pattern. The participation of the story in archetypal actions such as are inherent in the later Platonic fables, though it is different from that suggested in the prayers of Book III, is basic and shows up clearly in the action and the imagery used to describe it.

Even the participants' misapprehensions about the true status of the love experience in the cosmic plan are quite human and are themselves a part of the realism. An overestimation of the purity and purifying power of human love is a mark of the lover. The misapprehensions are not finally corrected till the Epilogue, and then are perhaps overcorrected. The citation of Macrobius at the beginning of the *Roman de la Rose* signals the poem's connection with the cosmic allegories, and the narration of Scipio's story prior to the dream in the *Parliament of Fowls* makes clear its participation in the genre. Inversely, the Macrobian journey of the soul of Troilus to the eighth sphere retrospectively marks the association of Chaucer's long poem with the genre. Instead of beginning with an overview of the universe and eventually narrowing to earthly activity, Chaucer only at the end of his story places it visually in the broad cosmic context. Troilus's damning of 'al oure werk' (V, 1823) at this point goes beyond even Scipio's scorn of the little earth, and we must allow even here for some dramatic overstatement. For the torch of Venus conveys a genuine heavenly spark to Troilus and Criseyde and to Amant and Fair Welcome in the *Roman*. Though misused, it is divine, and the poets, through presentations that have affecting realism, suggest the bit of divinity that is present.

That the *Roman de la Rose* led Chaucer to his use of the Arts of Love and the cosmic allegories in *Troilus and Criseyde* seems likely, but it is not certain. While the realistic elements that the two works owe to these literary families are similar, they are not at all identical. The parts of *Pamphilus* that show up in *Troilus* are somewhat different from those that the *Roman* incorporates, and Chaucer's story is at a further remove from the philosophical fables than the narrative of Guillaume and Jean. Moreover, the realism of *Troilus* appears quite like that of modern fiction, whereas that of the *Roman de la Rose* is obviously a medieval kind. The realism of *Troilus* is more complex, and it has other roots in literature that we have not dealt with here.

The attempt to specify and explicate the various literary strains – genres – that inform *Troilus* of course involves no attempt to deny Chaucer's originality. T. S. Eliot states, 'Not only the best, but the most individual parts of [a writer's] work may be those in which the dead poets, his ancestors, assert their immortality most vigorously'.[38] *Troilus and Criseyde* bears out this paradox. It is of its own kind – *sui generis* – not in spite of, but almost by virtue of, its participation in the several kinds of its predecessors.

Paganism and Pagan Love in *Troilus and Criseyde*

JOHN FRANKIS

Troilus and Criseyde reflects the common medieval ambivalence towards classical antiquity, in which veneration for the glories of ancient civilization contrasts with apprehension on behalf of those who had not been granted the Christian revelation and with doubts about the moral status of paganism. Virgil, for example, was acknowledged to be a poet of unsurpassed greatness as regards poetic technique, so great that God had chosen to speak through him in the Fourth Eclogue to prophesy the birth of Christ to the pagan world, but as a pagan Virgil was barred from entry into the heaven that was open to Christians:

> *chè quello Imperador, che lassù regna,*
> *perch'io fui ribellante alla sua legge,*
> *non vuol che in sua città per me si vegna.*[1]

Troilus was acknowledged to be a great lover and hero, but he likewise suffered from the limiting factor of his paganism; after death he is able to see this world from the viewpoint of eternity (V, 1807–25), but we are not told whether this is granted to all souls leaving this earth or whether it is a special concession to Troilus, or even a symbolic development of his earlier perceptiveness; then Mercury, in his classical role as *psychopompos*, conducts him to the place appointed for him:

> *And forth he wente, shortly for to telle,*
> *Ther as Mercurye sorted hym to dwelle.*
> (V, 1826–7)

Chaucer gives us no details of this place and no speculations about the eternal fate of pagans: this would be irrelevant to the poem, though orthodox views on the subject were presumably familiar to Chaucer and to many of his audience.[2]

The most prominent authorial statement on paganism is of course at the end of the poem, but the whole poem is saturated with references to Trojan paganism that do not reflect such an explicit authorial viewpoint; an ambiguous tone is set in the prologues to the first four books, while within the narrative Chaucer represents a society in which personal attitudes to religion vary from one individual to another. The conversation between Troilus and Pandarus in III, 701–40, exemplifies one aspect of Chaucer's technique: Troilus's speeches are full of appeals to the gods – Venus, Jove, Mars, Phoebus, Mercury, Diana and the Fates – while Pandarus's replies are scornful, realistic and practical; for example:

> 'Mercurie, for the love of Hierse eke,
> For which Pallas was with Aglawros wroth,
> Now help! and ek Diane, I the biseke,
> That this viage be nought to the looth.
> O fatal sustren, which, er any cloth
> Me shapen was, my destine me sponne,
> So helpeth to this werk that is bygonne!'
>
> Quod Pandarus, 'Thow wrecched mouses herte,
> Artow agast so that she wol the bite?'
>
> (III, 729–37)

What emerges from all this, however, is not an impression of a religious man conversing with a sceptic, but simply of a timid man who needs help contrasted with one who is confident of his own capacities in this field of activity. The fact that Troilus's remarks are pagan as opposed to Christian is not immediately relevant: the reader's initial response is a suspension of his disbelief in paganism in order to savour the comedy of a situation in which Troilus ascribes to pagan powers activities that are to be performed for him by Pandarus. The primary significance of the passage, that is to say, is its representation of character (in the sense of recognisable human behaviour patterns) rather than an evaluation of religious faith. When Pandarus is working to undermine Criseyde's resistance he too can appeal to the gods:

'For, nece, by the goddesse Mynerve,
And Jupiter, that maketh the thondre rynge,
And by the blisful Venus that I serve,
Ye ben the womman in this world lyvynge,
Withouten paramours, to my wyttynge,
That I best love . . .'

(II, 232–7)

but here too our response is in terms of character: we are amused by the man who can use religious expressions when it serves his purpose, but we are not shocked by any serious sense of hypocrisy, still less of blasphemy, nor do we disapprove of the expressions because they are pagan rather than Christian, for the rights and wrongs of paganism are not an issue at this point. Much of the pagan imagery in the poem is on this level: its primary function is to provide a kind of local colour, like many of the references to the events and heroes of the Trojan war. But just as the background of the war has in places a more serious and constructive function in the poem, so too there are passages in which the theme of paganism invites the reader's closer attention and more critical scrutiny, particularly when the narrator ascribes some power to the forces of paganism and obliges us to adopt a moral stance to this power. In such cases the pagan gods, as often in medieval writing, are represented not as powerless fictions but as actual forces with some capacity to influence human life, and their role can obviously not be dissociated from the influence of the planets that bear their names.

It is important that Troilus first catches sight of Criseyde in a pagan temple (I, 160–4): from its inception their love has a pagan element in it, and the fact that Criseyde is alone in Troy is due to Apollo's revelations to her father Calkas (I, 69–72): it is as if the gods had prepared the ground for the events of the story. The conversation between Troilus and Pandarus already mentioned (III, 701–40) is in fact encapsulated in a scene that may encourage a further interpretation in addition to that given above, for Chaucer in characteristic fashion allows for successive layers of meaning: this conversation, which on the face of it seems to imply the ineffectual nature of the pagan gods in that the important work is done by Pandarus, is placed in a wider context that affirms the power of the gods. Troilus's remarks, looked at from within the fiction, are a timid young man's plea for help formulated in conventional appeals to an established religion, but seen objectively they are also an appeal to

59

real powers that are actually at work at that moment, for the consummation of Troilus's love is not only due to the machinations of Pandarus, which in Book III reach a climax of farcicality that undermines our sense of the seriousness of the situation; it also depends on the support of the pagan powers that send a storm to prevent Criseyde from leaving Pandarus's house. There is a striking contrast between the two sets of activities: on one hand, Pandarus with the triviality of his secret trapdoor and his incessant officiousness that pushes the helpless Troilus from one indignity to another; and on the other hand, the gods with their powers manifested in the terrifying and deafening storm,

> *That every maner womman that was there*
> *Hadde of that smoky reyn a verray feere.*
> (III, 627–8)

The whole scene (III, 617–1190) is a masterpiece of comic writing, and its remarkable blending of the serious, the ominous and the absurd has an obvious appeal to our own time. The power behind the storm is initially named as Fortune (III, 617), but the events are then specified as the work of the Moon, Saturn and Jove (III, 624–5: Robinson's note on these lines comments on the significance of this conjunction of planets). The role of Jupiter 'that maketh the thondre rynge' is clear enough, but Saturn and the Moon play more complex parts; Saturn is the bringer of disaster (as in the Knight's Tale, 2456–69), and his involvement indicates that the ensuing events are not intended to have a happy outcome, while the Moon (Diana-Lucina) not only has the malice towards human beings that Chaucer normally ascribes to the pagan gods (in the Knight's Tale 2065–72 she seems to be concerned less with the preservation of chastity than with the punishment of those who offend her), but she also has in other works by Chaucer a particularly sinister aspect that appears in her association with the 'derke regioun' of the underworld (see the Knight's Tale, 2077–82, and the Franklin's Tale, 1074–5): the implication is, of course, that these powers will work to turn Troilus's love to disaster, and the pattern of their operations is indicated by their being placed together with Fortune, who blindly raises men up so as to cast them down again. The pagan gods with their storm may seem prepared to help the coming together of Troilus and Criseyde, but their favours, like Fortune's, are arbitrary and irresponsible, for they later seem to be equally prepared to encourage the coming

60

together of Criseyde and Diomede: the approach of the night during
which Criseyde first seriously considers the advantages of a liaison
with Diomede is described in terms of the activity of pagan planetary
deities in a way that is not solely metaphorical:

> *The brighte Venus folwede and ay taughte*
> *The wey ther brode Phebus down alighte;*
> *And Cynthea hire char-hors overraughte*
> *To whirle out of the Leoun, if she myghte;*
> *And Signifer his candels sheweth brighte,*
> *Whan that Criseyde unto hire bedde wente*
> *Inwith hire fadres faire brighte tente,*
>
> *Retornyng in hire soule ay up and down*
> *The wordes of this sodeyn Diomede.*
> (V, 1016–24)

The planetary imagery is of course a rhetorical description of the
coming of night, but the more positive contribution of the pagan
powers on this occasion becomes clear if one compares the treatment
of the theme of nightfall on the parallel occasion when Criseyde's
resistance to Troilus begins to weaken:

> *The dayes honour, and the hevenes ye,*
> *The nyghtes foo – al this clepe I the sonne –*
> *Gan westren faste, and downward for to wrye,*
> *As he that hadde his dayes cours yronne;*
> *And white thynges wexen dymme and donne*
> *For lak of lyght, and sterres for t'apere,*
> *That she and alle hire folk in went yfeere.*
> (II, 904–10)

In this passage not only is the rhetorical element undermined by the
deliberate facetiousness of the narrator's intrusion in the second line,
but the process of nightfall is represented as something natural,
familiar and, in the remarkably evocative imagery of lines 908–9,
attractive: symbolically, the development of Criseyde's love for
Troilus is natural and desirable. In the passage in Book V, however,
nightfall is, so to speak, contrived by the gods so as to give Criseyde a
nudge in the direction of Diomede.

When the power of the pagan gods has been established as part of
the total fiction, Criseyde's belittling of this power is clearly ominous,

61

even though the context of her words weakens much of their potential force:

> 'For goddes speken in amphibologies,
> And, for a sooth, they tellen twenty lyes.
> Eke drede fond first goddes, I suppose.'
>
> (IV, 1406–8)

We recognize the justice of this comment, both as regards Troilus's earlier expressions of piety in III, 701–40 (discussed above), which beautifully illustrate the principle of *Timor invenit deos*, and also as regards subsequent events in the story and Chaucer's condemnation of paganism at the end of the poem; but within the fiction we recognize the danger of such outspokenness and cynicism. In addition to their obvious dramatic irony, Criseyde's remarks also give us a criterion for evaluating her later promise to meet Troilus:

> 'And trusteth this, that certes, herte swete,
> Er Phebus suster, Lucina the sheene,
> The Leoun passe out of this Ariete,
> I wol ben here, withouten any wene.
> I mene, as helpe me Juno, hevenes quene,
> The tenthe day, but if that deth m'assaile,
> I wol yow sen, withouten any faille.'
>
> (IV, 1590–96)

Criseyde's promise to come on the tenth day is thus undermined by being made dependent on the co-operation of Diana and Juno: she seems to have forgotten her earlier distrust of the gods, but the reader has not, and we recognize that, albeit unwittingly, she speaks, like the gods, 'in amphibologies'.

Circumstances also lead Troilus to criticize the pagan gods:

> And in his throwes frenetik and madde
> He corseth Jove, Appollo, and ek Cupide,
> He corseth Ceres, Bacus, and Cipride . . .
>
> (V, 206–8)

This emotional outburst is of course a dramatic expression of character, but ironically Troilus's 'madde' rejection of the pagan gods marks a kind of advance in wisdom, and is supported by the author at the end of the poem. At a slightly later point, however, Troilus ascribes a different kind of power to a pagan god when he claims that Cupid's treatment of him is making him into a fit theme for a work of fiction:

> *Thanne thoughte he thus, 'O blisful lord Cupide,*
> *Whan I the proces have in my memorie,*
> *How thow me hast wereyed on every syde,*
> *Men myght a book make of it, lik a storie.'*
>
> (V, 582–5)

When Troilus sees himself as a character in a book as a result of the work of Cupid the imagery has multiple implications, not only as when a character in a play by Shakespeare compares himself to an actor on a stage (Troilus actually is a character in a book by virtue of his experience of love) but also because there is a suggestion of the relationship between love and poetry, Cupid–Venus and the Muses (as in the prologue and epilogue to Book III), which exemplifies Chaucer's constant awareness of his relationship to a long-standing poetic tradition. Troilus, within Chaucer's fiction, sees himself participating in this tradition and ascribes this to the pagan powers whose inspiration the narrator had invoked in the prologue to Book III. The overtly fictional aspect of Troilus is also mentioned in V, 267–73, where all mankind, and especially the narrator and audience, are called on to show sympathetic involvement in Troilus's sufferings, in marked contrast to the serene indifference of the planets that mark the passage of time in the following stanza (274–80), where Phoebus's 'rosy carte' is almost an affront to Troilus's agony.

Two of Troilus's speeches in praise of love have justly received a good deal of critical attention; they occur immediately before and after the consummation of his love (III, 1254–74, and 1744–71), and both show a breaking away from the conventional paganism of his world, or rather a penetration beyond it to something approaching an apprehension of the eternal God of Christianity. In these speeches, which mark the high point of Troilus's happiness, we see the tragedy of his situation: that he can see so much further than his fellow pagans, but that his paganism still makes his vision faulty. Troilus's confused groping after a knowledge beyond the conventional paganism of his age appears in the first of these speeches:

> *Than seyde he thus, 'O Love, O Charite!*
> *Thi moder ek, Citherea the swete,*
> *After thiself next heried be she,*
> *Venus mene I, the wel-willy planete!*

And next that, Imeneus, I the grete;
For nevere man was to yow goddes holde
As I, which ye han brought fro cares colde.'
                                                (III, 1254–60)

It is striking that here Charity (presumably *caritas*, the Christian virtue of, for example, I Corinthians xiii) is identified with Cupid, the son of Venus, 'the wel-willy planete', and the significance of the invocation to Hymen, the god of marriage, is debatable (see below). In the following stanza Troilus refers to love (presumably, in the first place, his feeling for Criseyde) as 'Benigne Love, thow holy bond of thynges', a term appropriate to the Christian concept of divine love, and the Christian associations of the lines that follow (1262–7) are obvious (they are in fact based on St Bernard's prayer to the Virgin Mary in Dante's *Paradiso*, xxxiii, 13–18). Troilus's claims that his love for Criseyde is a reflection or part of the divine love that binds creation together have frequently been discussed, and it is important to see that the references to pagan gods introduce a discordant note into his praise of love. Cupid and Venus are not allegories of Christian love: in other poems by Chaucer they are powers inimical to man and they are the cause of strife and division, as is made clear in the Temples of Venus in *The House of Fame*, *The Parliament of Fowls* and the Knight's Tale, and Troilus's attempt to identify them with eternal love shows how his paganism imposes limitations on his capacity to grasp the truth. This speech should in fact be evaluated in the light of the common medieval literary theme of the rivalry between Venus and Christ (or the Virgin Mary), between the religion of love and Christianity. This rivalry is further pointed at the end of Book III when the narrator addresses the pagan trinity at the centre of the cult of the religion of love – Venus, Cupid and the Muses: Mother, Son and Inspirers (III, 1807–13). This address, which recalls and balances the invocation to Venus and Calliope in the prologue to Book III, also indicates that the religion of love is a literary phenomenon; this is appropriate in utterances (the prologue and epilogue) that come from the narrator, for paradoxically, just as within the story Troilus moves in a quasi-real world of human relationships, so in the commentary the narrator treads a parallel path in a bookish world of the imagination, learning from what he relates and theorizing about it. Troilus's experience of love thus becomes a kind of education for the narrator, and so Troilus's inability to distinguish between the eternal (Christian) and transient (pagan) aspects of love finds at this point an echo in the narrator himself, for Troilus's second great praise of love (III, 1744–71) is markedly less pagan than the narrator's praise of Venus that follows it (III, 1807–20). Where the narrator gives us a celebration of the religion of love – 'Ye heried ben for ay withouten ende!' – Troilus gives us a Boethian hymn, in which a reference to Phoebus is an obvious metaphor in an unmistakably Christian context: indeed, where the Christian Boethius refers to Phoebus, Phoebe and Hesperus, Chaucer makes Troilus refer only to Phoebus (III, 1755: compare with *De Consolatione Philosophiae* II, metrum 8, 5–8), and the sequence of day and night appears as part of a beneficent natural order and not as an arbitrary contrivance of the gods. As has frequently been pointed out, however, Troilus's praise of love differs in one important detail from its source in Boethius, as a comparison with Chaucer's translation of *De Consolatione Philosophiae* makes quite clear; the relevant passages are as follows:

Chaucer's *Boece*, Bk. II, Met. 8, ll. 21–3	*Troilus* III, 1746–9
This love halt togidres peples	Love, that with an holsom al-liaunce
joyned with an hooly bond, and	Halt peples joyned, as hym lest hem gye,
knytteth sacrement of mariages	Love, that knetteth lawe of compaignie,
of chaste loves . . .	And couples doth in vertue for to dwelle . . .

In adapting this source for Troilus's praise of love Chaucer removes Boethius's reference to marriage as a manifestation of divine love and replaces it with a vague reference to 'the lawe of compaignie' and to dwelling in virtue. One might see here a discrepancy with Troilus's earlier praise of love, for in III, 1254–60, Troilus invokes not only Cupid and Venus but also Hymen, the god of marriage, perhaps implying that for Troilus at this point marriage is the concomitant of love, whereas by the end of Book III marriage has disappeared from Troilus's meditations. This discrepancy reflects the inconsistency of attitudes to marriage throughout the whole poem: the subject is not totally absent from the poem, but it is mentioned only rarely and indirectly. Criseyde is a widow (I, 97–8), which implies the existence of marriage in Chaucer's fictional world, and Helen, though never said to be married to Paris – merely ravished (I, 62) and fetched (V,

890) – is consistently described as sister to Paris's brothers Deiphebus (II, 1559), Troilus (II, 1572) and Hector (II, 1626–7), which implies a quasi-marital relationship, though Paris never appears in the poem. The theme of marriage as an institution, and particularly of marital relationships (so prominent elsewhere in Chaucer's writings), is never dealt with explicitly in *Troilus and Criseyde*: we hear a good deal of Hector, but nothing of Andromache, whose name would evoke memories of one of the classical ideals of marital devotion (see, for example, the Nun's Priest's Tale, 3141–9); we hear nothing of Priam and Hecuba as a married couple, and at no point in the poem are a husband and wife shown together. It is as if Chaucer wished to represent a society in which marriage has little significance and is virtually non-existent. Under stress Troilus can invoke a range of gods, Hymen among them, but his thinking is confused and it is as if he has not fully worked out the implications of his prayers. The evasive attitude to marriage in the poem also appears when Troilus, shocked by the news of the imminent exchange of Criseyde for Antenor, considers first abducting her then, apparently, marrying her; he has to reject both possibilities, of course, 'Syn she is chaunged for the townes good' (IV, 553), and to sabotage the exchange would be treason. Nevertheless, the apparent reference to marriage is oddly noncommittal and inexplicit:

> 'I have ek thought, so it were hire assent,
> To axe hire at my fader, of his grace;
> Than thynke I, this were hire accusement,
> Syn wel I woot I may hire nought purchace.
> For syn my fader, in so heigh a place
> As parlement, hath hire eschaunge enseled,
> He nyl for me his lettre be repeled.'
> (IV, 554–60)

For Chaucer's world the phrase 'To axe hire at my fader' would doubtless imply the Christian institution of marriage, but its implications for pagan Troy are left vague; clearly it implies some public acknowledgement and official recognition of a relationship between a man and woman, but Troilus thinks that this would be in some way compromising or discreditable to her – 'this were hire accusement' – but whether as a matter of personal morality (implying some impropriety on Criseyde's part) or as a matter of state politics (appearing to involve Criseyde in a conspiracy to sabotage the exchange) is not specified. The status of marriage in Chaucer's fictitious world of Trojan paganism is left unclear, but one notes that in general in this poem paganism does not seem to involve personal devotion or devoutness in the Christian understanding of those terms, and one might deduce that it rather encourages a concern with transient matters and trivialities, for Chaucer represents a certain lack of seriousness about ultimate issues among its devotees (there is no Theseus in Troy), and its gods show a corresponding lack of care for mankind. Troilus is perceptive enough to grasp something of the nature of human and divine love, of love as the motive power of the universe, the 'holy bond of thynges', 'L'amor che move il sole e l'altre stelle' (*Paradiso*, xxxiii, 145), but because of his paganism he hopes to approach this love through (and even to identify it with) Venus and Hymen. This is not a totally misconceived hope, for Troilus has to learn the lesson of love somehow, but it is partly illusory in so far as his society makes lavish provision for Venus but none very clearly for Hymen. That is to say, paganism as represented by Chaucer cannot sanctify and perpetuate human love because it lacks the sacrament of Holy Matrimony: all it can offer in place of the Christian *coniugii sacrum* (*De Cons. Phil.*, II, met. 8, line 24) is a vague hope about dwelling in virtue, and this is not powerful enough to perpetuate love. Troilus sees a connection between human and cosmic love, but his society does not provide a machinery for cementing this bond. The political circumstances that force the lovers apart would presumably have been irrelevant if Trojan society had encouraged Troilus to think in terms of marriage right from the start, but in this society the institution of marriage is represented as having no appeal to the imagination of the young. Troilus therefore loses Criseyde, and with her he seems to lose his capacity for comprehending cosmic love.

The fiction of a paganism that does not ordinarily allow for enduring marital happiness is one that Chaucer develops further in *The Canterbury Tales*, where there are details that may serve to clarify some aspects of *Troilus and Criseyde*. For some years now the Franklin's Tale has been the subject of dispute: formerly taken as implying charity and wisdom on the part of the devoted husband Arveragus (e.g. by Kittredge in his seminal article on the alleged 'marriage group'), it was later interpreted by D. W. Robertson as an attack on the shallowness and folly of both its hero and its narrator.[3] It is interesting to apply Professor Robertson's views on the Franklin's Tale to Chaucer's presumed source in Boccaccio's *Il Filocolo*, for there the story is set in medieval Italy (i.e. apparently in a Christian society) and the author's approval of the husband is more obvious and explicit, so that whatever Robertson has to say about Chaucer's Franklin might seem equally applicable to Boccaccio himself (which might of course lead us to question some of Robertson's judgements this tale).[4] However that may be, Chaucer changes the story in important ways: he transfers it to a pagan society and includes explicit condemnations of paganism, he makes marital relationship a far more prominent theme than it is in Boccaccio, and he encourages the reader to question the wisdom of Arveragus's decision (Franklin's Tale, 1493–8: to hear the end of the tale, of course, is not to hear how Arveragus is vindicated, but only to see how the moral issue is side-stepped). The marriage of Arveragus and Dorigen is invested from the beginning with a quasi-Christian standard of devotion and fidelity (see lines 758–60 and 789–90) and Dorigen's prayer is to a quasi-Christian God:

> *Eterne God that thurgh thy purveiance*
> *Ledest the world by certein governaunce.*
> (865–6)

Her God is moreover expected to care for his creation (lines 876–83). Explicitly pagan forces are introduced only when Aurelius wishes to disturb this quasi-Christian arrangement: he, of course, is a servant of Venus (937), and his prayer to Apollo (1031–79) stands in marked contrast to Dorigen's earlier prayer to the eternal God. The forces called upon by Aurelius to achieve his ends are condemned as pagan by the narrator:

> *. . . swich folye*
> *As in oure dayes is nat worth a flye,*
> *For hooly chirches feith in oure bileve*
> *Ne suffreth noon illusioun us to greve.*
> (1131–4)

Although the magic spells of the 'subtil clerk' are effective (at least as an illusion), they are scorned by the narrator because they are pagan:

> *. . . swiche illusiouns and swiche meschaunces*
> *As hethen folk useden in thilke dayes*
> (1292–3)

– words that recall Chaucer's denunciation of the cursed old rites of pagans at the end of *Troilus and Criseyde*. Dorigen's comment on the works of these pagan powers is revealing – 'It is agayns the proces of nature' (1345) – for the process of nature is the obvious earthly manifestation of the eternal God of order to whom she had earlier prayed. We read in *Mandeville's Travels*, for example, that when Alexander the Great invoked the God of Nature his prayer was granted because, in spite of Alexander's paganism, it was taken to be addressed to the eternal God of Christian teaching, so Alexander's faith in a natural order actually moved mountains.[5] Dorigen thus aligns herself with the true God against the forces of paganism, and the end of the tale may be regarded as a re-establishment of divine order symbolized, as so often in romantic comedy, in the state of marriage, though the tale is admittedly not presented in this way; there is consequently something of a discrepancy between the strongly Chaucerian portion (down to about line 1500), with its emphasis on the moral issues of paganism and marriage, and the Boccaccio-like ending from which these issues are dropped.

Marriage as a symbol, or even a manifestation, of divine order is of course even more explicitly expounded in the Knight's Tale, and here too it is set in opposition to the forces of paganism. The anti-human nature of the pagan gods is amply illustrated in the descriptions of the temples of Venus, Mars and Diana, as well as in Saturn's device for reconciling the conflicting demands of the junior deities; and when Theseus wishes to establish a state of divine order on earth he invokes, like Dorigen and Alexander, a power of natural order that corresponds to the eternal God of Christianity, as is clearly indicated in the terms of his speech (Knight's Tale, 2987–3016). The defeat of the pagan gods has already been foreshadowed in the flight of the woodland deities when the trees are felled for Arcite's funeral pyre (2925–8) and Theseus's speech predicts the subordination of Saturn and his fellow gods to the one eternal God in terms of the replacement of disorder by order. (That Theseus goes on in line 3035 to name the one eternal God as Jupiter potentially confuses the issue, but the context makes the situation clear: Saturn, Mars, Venus and Diana represent powers of chaos inimical to man, while, in this tale, Jupiter stands allegorically for the eternal God of order, justice and divine love.) The restoration of divine order on earth is manifested in the joining of Palamon and Emily in 'the bond / That highte matri-moigne or mariage' (3094–5). Marriage is the proper ending for a romantic comedy, for the Christian institution of Holy Matrimony symbolizes and reflects divine love and order; the Christian sacrament was not available to a pagan world, but in the Knight's Tale, and less certainly in the Franklin's Tale, Chaucer seems to imply that the Christian god might on occasion intervene to thwart the malevolent pagan powers, particularly if appealed to in the name of the process of nature and eternal order. It might be felt that Troilus's invocation of love in *Troilus and Criseyde*, III, 1744–71, constitutes such an appeal, for, like Dorigen, Theseus and Alexander, Troilus has the capacity to see beyond the pagan gods to an unchanging eternal power that binds the universe together in harmony; but each of Chaucer's poems establishes its own conventions and its own myths, and what is appropriate to a comedy may not serve in a tragedy. When Troilus's hymn to love at the end of Book III draws on Boethian terms that are appropriate to Christian faith, it has to exclude the reference to the function of marriage, for in pagan Troy there is no divine intervention to render earthly love permanent within the term of human life; Troilus may have been able to see beyond earthly love to divine love, but one aspect of his tragedy is that the world he lives in seems not to allow for marriage as a way of sanctifying love. (His tragedy obviously has other aspects too, including the force of circumstances and the nature of Criseyde herself: the poem is richly compounded of numerous strands.) The impermanence of Troilus's relationship with Criseyde is particularly tragic since it seems that Troilus's capacity to apprehend the eternal principle of cosmic order that operates through divine love cannot survive the loss of Criseyde, for human love is the basis of his sense of divine love: without the former he cannot retain the latter. Part of the appeal of the poem lies in the fact that beside its religious attitudes, implicit at various points throughout and uniquely explicit at the end, there is a contrasting humanist element. Troilus's devotion to Criseyde leads him to some understanding of cosmic love, but there is no ascent of any Platonic ladder on which a higher love replaces a lower. Troilus's sense of divine love does not transcend or sublimate his human love, it cannot even be a substitute for it, because for Troilus there is no substitute for the happiness of fulfilled human love. One is reminded of the implications of one of Chaucer's earliest poems: when a loved person dies the Christian can find consolation (as the dreamer in *Pearl* does) in the belief that the dead person has gone to a happier life in a better world, but the dreamer in *The Book of the Duchess* in the last resort offers no such consolation: he accepts that the loss caused by death is irreparable, that a human being is unique and irreplaceable, so that the poem is concerned not with the comforts of religion, real though they may be, but with expounding the nature of bereavement. Chaucer was not a sceptical humanist, and we need not doubt his Christian faith, but he seems to have had a sense of the value and uniqueness of earthly human relationships, especially between man and woman, while being prepared to acknowledge their transient aspects. The Christian will presumably assert that eternal life cannot be imperfect and lacking in something essential, even though 'in the resurrection they neither marry nor are given in marriage' (Matthew xxii. 30); but the pagan Troilus neither sees nor desires any heavenly alternative to human love: when he has lost Criseyde, he cannot continue his pursuit of a higher love, for his concept of love is human-centred. Having no heavenly consolation to turn to, Troilus devotes himself instead to the pursuit of vengeance and dies in battle (V, 1800–6). His vision from the eighth sphere enables him to disdain the world and to understand the nature of true happiness, but this restoration of something like his earlier cosmic view is more in the nature of a gift than an achievement. As Troilus is led off by Mercury into whatever eternity is appointed for him, the narrator treads a parallel but different path; he has received enlightenment by retelling the story of Troilus's joy and suffering, and the enlightenment has grown as the story has developed. The supreme happiness of fulfilled love in Book III leads Troilus to a partial perception beyond the limits of his paganism, but paradoxically enthusiasm for Troilus's bliss leads the narrator to an intensified admiration for the pagan powers that he holds responsible for this bliss, as appears in the invocation to Venus in the epilogue (III, 1807–20). As the course of the tragedy goes on to reveal more of the unreliability and duplicity of the pagan gods, however, the narrator, following his hero and suffering with him, turns his mind to contempt of the world and of all the transient things that the pagan gods represent; finally he rediscovers his own religion under the influence of Troilus's vision after death and affirms the Christian hope of eternity (V, 1835–48), contrasting this hope with the hopelessness of paganism and the worthlessness of its gods:

> Lo here, of payens corsed olde rites,
> Lo here, what alle hire goddes may availle;
> Lo here, thise wrecched worldes appetites;
> Lo here, the fyn and guerdon for travaille
> Of Jove, Appollo, of Mars, of swich rascaille!
> (V, 1849–53)

Troilus's tragedy is a tragedy of suffering and loss, but it is also the tragedy of paganism in that for the pagan there can (at least in this poem) be no divine comedy ending in paradise. Perhaps because the life of the pagan is so earth-centred the Christian narrator can learn

71

something of the human condition by telling the story of a pagan, but though the narrator may enter into the experiences of his hero, even to the extent of sharing momentarily in his paganism, he is all the time on a different path; and however much this path may rise and fall with the career of the hero, it still has a different destination. The story of Troilus is essentially an affirmation of the unique value and irreplaceable nature of human earthly experience: this is certainly how it appears in the humanist versions of Boccaccio and Shakespeare, different though they are from each other. To say at the end of such a story, 'Do not attach any value to these trivial and transitory things, think of eternity!' might seem irrelevant and even inhuman, and many critics earlier in this century felt that Chaucer's ending was inappropriate. By putting this humanist story into the mouth of a Christian narrator, however, Chaucer can quite sincerely assert the triviality and transience of various aspects of human experience, while leaving with the reader an impression of the lasting value of these same things. Thus Chaucer creates a multi-layered poem that contains a complex of comments on the story itself, on the world of the ancients, on paganism as a myth of mankind without God, on the evaluation of experience and on the relationship of poetry and experience.

Letters as a Type of the Formal Level in
Troilus and Criseyde

JOHN McKINNELL

The concept of variation of narrative levels in medieval literature, and particularly in Chaucer, is now a familiar one. We have become accustomed to the idea that the narrative voice sometimes relates events as though they were present to us and speaks with the voices of the characters; at other times we hear a Narrator who is not the poet himself, and at others again we may think (though I doubt whether we can ever be sure) that we are meeting the views of the historical Geoffrey Chaucer. The idea has been put in varying ways, and is in essence very ancient. The germ of it can be seen in the commentary on Seneca's *Hercules Furens* made by Nicholas Trivet about 1315, which Chaucer may have known:

> Ex dictis autem patent quatuor cause huius tragedie, quia causa efficiens fuit Seneca, causa materialis est furia Herculis in qua interfecit filios et uxorem; causa formalis consistit in modo scribendi, qui est dragmaticus, ut dictum est, et ordine partium, qui patebit in expositione; causa finalis est delectatio populi audientis; vel in quantum hic narrantur quedam laude digna, quedam vituperio, potest aliquo modo liber hic supponi ethice, et tunc finis eius est correctio morum per exempla hic posita.

> However, from what has been said, four causes of this tragedy are apparent, for the effecting cause was Seneca; the material cause is the madness of Hercules in which he killed his sons and

wife; the formal cause consists in the type of writing, which is dramatic, as has been said, and in the arrangement of parts, which will appear in the (following) exposition; the final cause is the pleasure of the listening audience, or in so much as there are here narrated some things worthy of praise and some of blame, the book may alternatively be regarded morally, and then its end is the correction of behaviour by the examples presented here.[1]

As Chaucer explicitly calls *Troilus and Criseyde* a tragedy (V, 1786*),[2] Trivet's classification may be valid for it too. In that case, the 'material cause' is obviously the narrative fiction and the 'final cause' the author's final intention; and as Trivet proceeds in his next section to portray the poet as a performing narrator, his 'effecting cause' seems roughly equivalent to the level of the narrator. True, Trivet does not make explicit the fictional nature of the narrator's persona, but in this respect Chaucer's narrators are an extreme case; some of his contemporaries produced narrators whose fictional status is questionable (e.g. Dante and Guillaume de Machaut), and his followers in English, like King James I and Hoccleve, often portray narrators whose pronounced individuality can only be explained as portrayal of the authors themselves.

But this still leaves Trivet's 'formal cause' unaccounted for. Here he seems to create an appearance of philosophical neatness by cramming two ideas into the same Aristotelian category, and a translation into modern critical terms would render the 'formal cause' as both

(a) the interaction between levels and between the effect of the work and the expectations of its audience for that genre, and
(b) the idea that individual sections (analysed by Trivet as *carmina*) may separately reflect new light on the work as a whole.

The two ideas are related, because the ability of individual *carmina* to reflect on the whole work depends on their autonomy of level or 'cause', and this autonomy is largely conferred by the genre expectations operating on each *carmen*, as itself rather than as part of a greater whole. Thus when Troilus offers us a courtly song, we should evaluate it first as a courtly song, and only after that in relation to him. Similarly, the dreams, letters and prayers in *Troilus and Criseyde* may contribute to a further level within the work, but only when they are first considered in relation to contemporary expectations of the types to which they belong. I am arguing, then, that beneath the familiar levels of narrative, narrator and author there is a localised and fragmented formal level, which can provide significant commentary on the other levels because the elements which make it up arouse their individual expectations, and that the strategy of employing this level had already been formulated by Chaucer's time in an important work on tragedy which he is likely to have known.

In post-medieval literature, deliberate alternation between levels has become unusual, and the bold spirits who have alternated the levels of fiction and narrator – Fielding, Byron, Trollope, among others – have done so largely for comic purposes. (I do not count the autobiographical novel, which usually creates only one level, absorbing the pseudo-narrator into the action. Only where the autobiographical narrator has become markedly different from the 'self' he portrays in the action, as with Conrad's Marlow in *Youth*, may there be alternation between levels, and even in *Youth* the case is doubtful and the effect somewhat sporadic.) And even these slight excursions into artifice were a source of disquiet to some of the best critical minds of the time, like Henry James, whose criticism of Trollope for reminding his readers of his own persona as novelist describes these reminders as 'discouraging', 'inexplicable' and 'deliberately inartistic'.[3]

Were it not that the 'intentional fallacy' has made cowards of us all, one would have expected someone to have asked, by now, the reason for this inhibition over the use of a device which lies at the heart of the achievement of many medieval poets. I wish to suggest that the major reason is that the medieval poet was writing chiefly for performance, whereas his more modern counterpart has used the mechanical medium of print, which can be quickly forgotten by his reader and through which rapid transition to a single world of imagination is possible. Here, an independent narrator would often be an annoying distraction, and attention tends to focus exclusively on the fictional action, even to the extent of implying that it had an existence of its own before the reader came on the scene – hence Tennyson's '*So* all day long the noise of battle rolled' and Matthew Arnold's '*And* the sun rose out of the Oxus stream'. A medieval performer who began in such a way would have seemed merely confusing; equally, the medium through which the poet then worked was a living reciter, of whose existence the audience might be reminded at any moment by something as trivial as an unexpected gesture or intonation. Since he could not be forgotten, it was desirable to create a role for him by dramatizing his relationship to his subject matter, and it was then easy to extend the principle of alternation of levels to provide variety or linking devices, and thereby hold the attention of a relatively captive audience.

This is not the place for a detailed refutation of the view that Chaucer and his contemporaries wrote solely or mainly for the silent reader, though I think such a refutation would be possible. But a few rhetorical questions may do to be going on with. Corpus Christi Cambridge MS 61 (of *Troilus and Criseyde*) has as its frontispiece a miniature of Chaucer reading aloud to an audience including Richard II and his court – could one imagine a similar picture of T. S. Eliot reading *The Waste Land* in the presence of King George V? Again, Davis's recent edition of the Paston Letters has demonstrated beyond reasonable doubt that most ladies of the knightly class were largely illiterate[4] – are we to assume, then, despite Chaucer's address to the ladies (*Troilus and Criseyde*, V, 1772–85*), that his intended audience was almost wholly male, and restricted to those who could read fluently (as not all gentlemen probably could)? Finally, how did the peasants of Kent acquire the knowledge of Langland necessary to understand John Ball's subversive letter of 1381?[5] It can hardly have been from manuscripts, which few of them could either have read or afforded. These are random instances, but they justify, at least as a working hypothesis, the contention that poetic works of Chaucer's time are primarily scripts for performance.

The major types which make up the formal level of *Troilus and Criseyde* – songs, dreams, prayers and letters – may be examined separately, and the rest of this article will concentrate on the last, which is in some respects the most difficult. It might be objected to the investigation of the letters, first that a performed work is ill equipped to portray them, as pre-eminently written documents; second, that in *Troilus and Criseyde* they have a narrative function which is not shared by songs, dreams or prayers, and that this restricted the poet's liberty in handling them; and third, that unlike the other elements of the formal level, most of them have specific originals in Boccaccio's *Il Filostrato*, so that Chaucer's individuality does not emerge strongly in them. The second and third of these must be admitted to some extent, but the latter part of this article will try to show that Chaucer's modifications of the letters in *Il Filostrato* are extensive, and that their function in the work is often radically altered. But the view that letters, as 'written evidence', were unsuited to a performed work, is mistaken, for real life letters were regarded chiefly as a storing of the spoken word. Most writers on *dictamen*, the art of letter writing, take this for granted, but at least one makes it explicit:

> Et dictamen dicitur eo quod dictatum in mente intellectum exprimat in voce.

> And *dictamen* is the name given to what the intellect, having composed it in the mind, expresses vocally.
> (Ludolf von Hildesheim, *Summa dictaminum*)

Ludolf also explains the origin of letter writing as a substitute for oral communication:

> Invencio autem literarum ortum habuit ab hiis qui voluntatem suam absentibus esse voluerunt manifestam. Et quia viva voce inmediate eis loqui non poterant, oportuit ut aliquo medio loquerentur. Causa autem invencionis literarum fuit negligencia nunciorum et ocultacio secretorum.

> The discovery of letters originated from those who wanted their wishes to be clear to those who were absent from them, and because they could not speak aloud to them without an inter-mediary, it was necessary for them to speak by some other means. However, the cause of the discovery of letters was the negligence of oral messengers and the (need for) concealment of secrets.[6]

A survey of the MS hands of the Paston Letters reinforces this view. Its most characteristic writers of autograph letters are servants, tenants and the like (163 autograph letters, 7 non-autograph, of which 2 have autograph signatures, and 12 doubtful)[7] and clerics (excluding bishops) (39 autograph letters, 7 non-autograph, of which 5 have autograph signatures, and 10 doubtful) – the sorts of people who rarely had any alternative to writing for themselves. But noblemen (including royalty and bishops) rarely wrote in their own hands, though their many autograph signatures suggest that this reflects choice, not necessity (7 autograph letters, 67 non-autograph, including 48 with autograph signatures, 3 doubtful).

The practice of the male gentry (including the Pastons themselves, and their social equals) shows an interesting change about 1460. Correspondents who began writing before that date have left 54 wholly or partly autograph letters, 93 non-autograph, only 16 with autograph signatures, and 4 doubtful; some of these autograph writers clearly wrote rather laboriously (e.g. John Paston I), and a few correspondents may have been illiterate (e.g. Sir John Fastolf, from whom there are 30 letters, 29 non-autograph and one doubtful).

But in gentlemen correspondents beginning in or after 1460, autograph letters become the rule except for legal affairs (187 wholly or partly autograph letters, 29 non-autograph, including 12 with autograph signatures, and 8 doubtful), but whatever the reason for this, general practice among the gentry in Chaucer's time is likely to have resembled that of the earlier Paston Letters.

Women correspondents must be considered separately. They show only one autograph letter, an ill-written and oddly spelt note from Elizabeth, Duchess of Suffolk, written between 1479 and 1483,[8] against 159 non-autograph letters, of which 11 have autograph signatures, and 10 doubtful cases. Many female correspondents were probably illiterate; thus Margery Brews, in the first of her two 'Valentine' letters to John Paston III,[9] says 'And I besech ȝowe ᵽat this bill be not seyn of non erthely creature safe only ȝour-selfe', but the hand is that of her father's clerk, Thomas Kela. Some of the Paston women could probably read however, even if they could write little; in no. 352[10] it is recorded that Anne Paston has lent a copy of Lydgate's *Siege of Thebes* to the Earl of Arran. This could have been read aloud to her, but Agnes Paston's will (1510) includes two prayer books, both bequeathed to women, and one 'keuered with redde and having a siluer claspe', which suggests a book for her personal use.[11] But it must be added that the other three wills of women in the family contain no books, and most of the evidence for female literacy occurs late in the period covered by the collection.

From this survey it can be seen that people who had the choice generally dictated their letters rather than writing themselves, at least in the period closest to Chaucer's time, and that illiteracy among those who could command the services of a scribe was no bar to letter writing; the idea of a letter as storage of the *spoken* word seems, therefore, to correspond with actual practice.

The surviving *artes dictandi* are very numerous; Rockinger's collection includes twenty works, all dating from Chaucer's time or earlier, and his list is not exhaustive.[12] Most are concerned primarily and many exclusively with official letters, for the study was often a means towards rapid promotion in the administration of Church or State. But an anonymous work formerly attributed to Alberich of Monte Cassino,[13] but written in Bologna c.1135, is a major source for many of the others, and some follow this in including examples of parts of personal letters; and John of Garland gives advice on letters as part of a larger work on writing in general. Both display considerable clarity and flexibility, and their advice was apparently not intended only for those who wanted to write in Latin; thus Guido Faba[14] (writing c.1230) includes examples in his native Italian as well as in Latin, and finds it unnecessary to justify this procedure.

Chaucer never mentions any writer on *dictamen*, and although he must have received a thorough training in the subject before he could become a civil servant and diplomat, it seems to have been usual in England to obtain such a training rather from Italian collections of specimen letters than from the *artes dictandi* themselves.[15] However, this distinction may not be a very real one, for even if he learned from specimen collections rather than from the *artes dictandi*, we may still expect Chaucer to show a familiarity with the traditional methods, which remained largely the same from one writer to another.

The simplest exposition of these outlines is probably that by the pseudo-Alberich *Rationes Dictandi*[16] mentioned above. This divides a letter into five parts:

1. *Salutatio* – the greeting. Its style should be appropriate to the rank of the person to whom the letter is sent, the sender is to express his name humbly, and it should come after the name of the recipient.
2. *Benevolentiae captatio* (called *exordium* by some writers) – an attempt to gain the sympathies of the recipient, by praising him and/or expressing one's own humility, invoking a special relationship, or making some offer. Most of the *benevolentiae captatio* can, it is stated, often be included in the *salutatio*.
3. *Narratio* – an explanation of something done, being done, or about to be done, or of a state of affairs. It may be either *simplex*, concerned with only one thing, or *multiplex*, with more than one.
4. *Peticio* – a request; this may also be either *simplex* or *multiplex*, and has nine sub-types, according to its tone – *deprecativa* (pleading), *preceptiva* (didactic), *conminativa* (threatening), *exhortatoria* (exhorting), *hortoria* (encouraging or inciting), *ammonitoria* (warning), *consultoria* (advising), *correptoria* (chiding), and *absoluta* (the mere request).
5. *Conclusio* – conclusion. This may be a logical conclusion or a summary. The *peticio* may here be reinforced by promises of favour if the request is granted (*affirmando*), or the reverse if it is not (*negando*).

There follows an outline of which parts may be removed from the scheme; thus the *salutatio* and *benevolentiae captatio* may be omitted when one wishes to insult or is afraid of having the letter intercepted;

the *peticio* is omitted when one does not wish to ask for anything. But every letter must contain either a *narrratio* or a *peticio*.

Details are then given of how the basic order of parts may be varied. One may move the *benevolentiae captatio* to immediately before the *peticio*, so that it may have the maximum effect on one's request; or (usually in replies) after the *peticio*, for example to soften a refusal. The *peticio* may precede the *narratio*, so that the latter may act as a supporting argument, but this cannot be done when one is *simplex* and the other *multiplex*. Where both are *multiplex*, and each part of the *peticio* is related to a particular part of the *narratio*, they may alternate.

But it may be hard to decide whether a writer knew this scheme or not, for some of it is common sense which a good writer might work out for himself, and its flexibility of attitude allows a wide range of differing but sensible plans to be included in it. But in the case of Boccaccio's *Il Filostrato*, this problem can be overcome. Here, three letters are given verbatim,[17] and all three follow the same basic pattern, with only very minor deviations; the chief of these is a tendency for the *benevolentiae captatio* to be included in the *salutatio* – which, as we have seen, is permitted by the *artes dictandi*. More conclusively, Boccaccio explicitly points out the only instance where he departs from the rules (in Troilo's naming himself first and refusing to greet his lady, in his first letter): '. . . ond' io mi scosto / Da quel che fanno gli altri' – 'Therefore I am departing from the practice of others'[18] – and this suggests strongly that he knew what the rules were.

In *Troilus and Criseyde*, only two letters are given verbatim (Troilus's in Book V, 1317–1421, based on *Il Fil.* VII, stt. 52–75; and Criseyde's in V, 1590–1631, which is original) although the summary of Troilus's first letter (II, 1065–84) is full enough for a rough analysis to be possible. Criseyde's last letter is perfectly conventional (though Chaucer, like Boccaccio, absorbs the *benevolentiae captatio* into the *salutatio*); but both Troilus's letters show interesting deviations from the permitted patterns, and we must try to decide whether these are deliberate portrayal of Troilus, or merely indicate that Chaucer's knowledge of *dictamen* was not very exact.

The first pair of letters, Troilus's avowal of love (II, 1065–84) and Criseyde's reply (II, 1221–5), are both written at the prompting of Pandarus and given in summary by Chaucer, as against long verbatim prototypes in *Il Filostrato* (II, stt. 96–106 and 121–7). There, both the manner of Pandaro's suggestion to Troilo that he write a letter and his letter itself are largely conventional; the suggestion merely advises Troilo to tell all his love and ask for pity, with the assurance that the outcome will be favourable (*Il Fil.* II, stt. 91–2). Troilo begins by *not* greeting his lady, saying that he is too miserable to greet anyone (a good striking *salutatio* in fact), and goes on to announce how he is compelled to write by Love (*narratio*, stt. 98–100), before throwing himself on Criseida's mercy (*peticio*, stt. 101–4) and concluding with two stanzas of *conclusio affirmando*. But in *Troilus and Criseyde*, the seriousness with which the conventions are viewed begins to be undermined when Pandarus helpfully adds some hints on how Troilus should set about it:

> 'Biblotte it with thi teris ek a lite;
> And if thow write a goodly word al softe,
> Though it be good, reherce it nought to ofte.'
> (II, 1027–9*)

The Narrator is similarly detached in his cheerful summary of Troilus's letter:

> 'First he gan hire his righte lady calle,
> His hertes lif, his lust, his sorwes leche,
> His blisse, and ek thise other termes alle
> That in swich cas thise loveres alle seche;
> (II, 1065–8*)

This, of course, serves both as *salutatio* and as *benevolentiae captatio*. But next comes the *peticio* (II, 1072–6) followed by another *benevolentiae captatio* (1077–81) emphasising his unworthiness. Then comes the *narratio* – 'his woo' (1082), before the simple *conclusio* (1084). But the *peticio* is allowed to precede the *narratio* only when the latter becomes an immediate supporting argument for it, and the second, intervening *benevolentiae captatio* disrupts that essential link. One must conclude either that Chaucer muddled a sequence which was completely 'correct' in his source, or else that Troilus shows a naïve inability to handle the letter form correctly.

A humorous attitude also colours the Narrator's attitude to Troilus's writing of the letter. When Troilus deprecates his own worth, the Narrator breaks in to say explicitly that he is lying (II, 1077–8*), and there is another hint of posturing when Troilus reads the letter over: 'And radde it over, and gan the lettre folde' (II, 1085). Followed by the pause of the stanza-ending, this creates the suggestion of finality and deliberation, as if he were savouring what he has just written. (Troilo doesn't read his letter over, and he folds it at the *beginning* of a stanza.)[19] Again, the piteous tone of the letter is belied by the eagerness and dexterity with which Troilus sets his seal on it (II, 1088*). These hints suggest a suppressed hopefulness – that in a sense he is even enjoying himself. A new atmosphere of slightly comic posturing therefore surrounds the conventional details, like the bathing of the ruby signet ring in his tears, which are taken over unchanged from *Il Filostrato*.

Criseyde's summarised reply is quite different from that of Boccaccio's heroine (*Il Filostrato*, II, stt. 121–7) which is a mixture of flattery of Troilo, self-deprecation, lip-service to chastity and discretion, and hints (which Troilo is quick to recognise, *Il Filostrato*, II, st. 129) that he may hope to find more specific favour in the not too distant future. Criseyde's brief reply is candour itself by contrast (II, 1221–5*), but if the summary of the letter itself reads like a seriously admirable mixture of charity and good sense (apart from the possibility of a sinister pun on *fayn* in II, 1225*), neither the scene out of which it comes nor the attitude of the Narrator conveys the same feeling. The Narrator contrives in quick succession to be pedantic and *faux naif*, using first the metaphor of the 'prison of disdain':

> She wente allone, and gan hire herte unfettre
> Out of desdaynes prison but a lite,
>
> (II, 1216–7*)

where even the conventional statement is made tentative by the final phrase. Then the Narrator alludes to the gulf between his aims and his capabilities:

> Of which to telle in short is myn entente
> Th' effect, as fer as I kan understonde.
>
> (II, 1219–20*)

If we are meant to take Criseyde's letter seriously, this intrusion seems tactless, since it draws our attention to him and away from his heroine; but a closer look at the scene suggests that this may be deliberate. The evidence of female correspondents in the Paston Letters may prompt us to accept Criseyde's protestation that she has never written a letter before (II, 1213–4*), even if Helen's capitulation to Paris in Ovid's *Heroides* (XVII, 143–4) is coyly peeping out at us under cover of it. But Criseyde's words to Pandarus after writing the letter cannot possibly be taken seriously:

. . . 'As wisly help me God the grete,
I nevere dide thing with more peyne
Than writen this, to which ye me constreyne;'

And took it hym.

(II, 1230–3*)

where the pause between stanzas emphasises the contrast between her protestation and her action in giving him the letter. Pandarus, too, is playing a game of contrast between statement and intention – he may look perfectly casual 'Ther as he sat and loked into the strete' (II, 1227*), but Criseyde did not hear his scheming instruction to Troilus a couple of hundred lines earlier:

'And thow shalt fynde us, if I may, sittynge
At som wyndow, into the strete lokynge.'

(II, 1014–5*)

He now has to make a sententious speech of a couple of stanzas to keep her at the window until, much to his and the Narrator's affected surprise:

. . . right as they declamed this matere,
Lo, Troilus, right at the stretes ende,

(II, 1247–8*)

The rather pompous *declamed* is applied to Criseyde as well as Pandarus; she has no real reason to expect that Troilus might appear at this point, except that much the same thing has happened before (II, 610 ff.*); as it is, perhaps she half hopes that he will.

Clearly, the Narrator is encouraging his listeners to view both letters with a cheerful detachment. Troilus's letter, like so many of his actions, shows an uncritical yet unspontaneous acceptance of courtly convention – he does not see its absurdities, even though it takes Pandarus to suggest to him both the letter and its general tone. Criseyde's reply is full of rather conventional good sense, but the touches of humour suggest that she is not wholehearted about it, and perhaps does not fully understand the reasons for it. In both cases, the Narrator works in a direction quite opposite to his more usual device of covering up the mistakes of his characters and persuading his audience to accept them. Here, he points out the mistakes, but in such a way as to disarm more serious criticism, to contrive the suggestion that the mistakes are all part of a game, and that the future lovers are endearing even in error.

The other four letters, all in Book V, make up a symmetrical group, roughly parallel to the earlier pair but quite different in tone. Troilus's first in this group (V, 1317–421), given verbatim, is based on a very long letter in *Il Filostrato* (VII, stt. 52–75); Criseyde's summarised reply (V, 1423–31) corresponds to that of Boccaccio's heroine (*Il Fil.*, VII, st. 105) except in a few details, whose effect is to remove the strong sense of the insincerity of Boccaccio's heroine.[20] Both poets then say that Troilus often wrote to her again (V, 1583–6; *Il Fil.*, VIII, st. 3), but Boccaccio also makes his hero send Pandaro to Criseida in the Greek camp every time there is a truce, to try to persuade her to return. Chaucer's removing this makes Criseyde more remote and allows Pandarus a rueful detachment in Book V, which seems rather out of place in *Il Filostrato* (V, st. 49), where Pandaro is still actively working on Troilo's behalf. In *Il Filostrato*, Criseida makes no further reply,[21] but Chaucer gives a verbatim answer which his Narrator supposes her to have written out of pity (V, 1590–1631*).

Troilus's verbatim letter is again abnormal in structure and style. It begins with the usual combination of *salutatio* and *benevolentiae captatio* (V, 1317–23), but goes on to alternate *narratio* (1324–37 and 1366–79) with *peticio* (1338–65 and 1380–1407) before a summary conclusion (1408–21). The pseudo-Alberich scheme admittedly says that *narratio* and *peticio* may alternate where both are *multiplex* and specific parts of each are particularly related to each other (ch. 11); but that is not the case here. Troilus's *narratio* is simple – his misery – and so is his *peticio* – the request that Criseyde return – so the alternation is merely confused.

The devices of *ars grammatica* are also used in an awkward, tortured way. Parentheses are frequent and sometimes long – the first stanza does not reach the bulk of its principal clause until the last line, and the third, beginning with a parenthesis in every line:

> 'For which to yow, <u>with dredful herte trewe</u>,
> I write, <u>as he that sorwe drifth to write</u>,
> My wo, <u>that everich houre encresseth newe</u>,
> Compleyning, <u>as I dar or kan endite</u>.'
> (V, 1331–4, my underlining)

disappears completely into an aside thereafter. The rhetorical use of the relative pronoun as a linking device[22] is overdone here (V, 1331,* 1359,* 1371,* 1373,* 1380*) and sometimes otiose ('the whos welfare' (V, 1359*) means simply 'your welfare') or ambiguous (the referant of *which* in 1380* is vague). The conventional paradox of V,

1375–9* is undermined by its last line: 'Everich joie or ese in his contrarie' (V, 1379*) which, by pointing it out, erodes the confident poise on which such a device relies. Repetition is used clumsily (e.g. V, 1348–51*), and the first half of the letter gives an effect of tortured perplexity very like that found by Patch in his analysis of Troilus's bungling, pseudo–Boethian soliloquy about Predestination (IV, 958–1078*). This sets the tone of the letter, but the second half, which is clearer and contains hardly any rhetorical inelegance, does include most of the comment on the positions of the lovers. This suggests that the ponderous, misapplied rhetoric of the first part and the faulty construction of the letter are a deliberate portrayal of Troilus's mental state.

This letter is shorter than its prototype, and Chaucer's hero adopts a more loving attitude, adding good wishes for Criseyde's welfare and, ironically, her honour (V, 1359–63*). Some of its force, like the dilemma of the betrayed lover, is taken over from Boccaccio:

> 'If any servant dorste or oughte of right
> Upon his lady pitously compleyne,
> Thanne wene I that ich oughte be that wight,'
>   (V, 1345–7)

But no courtly 'servant' may complain against his lady, and Chaucer has clarified Troilus's dilemma by removing a number of reproaches which make Troilo's letter inconsistent in this respect.[23] The one reproach which he adds has, oddly, the effect of reinforcing our sympathy with Criseyde:–

> '. . . and though no manere routhe
> Commeve yow, yet thynketh on youre trouthe.'
>   (V, 1385–6*)

because it is clearly induced by self-pity.

Some of Chaucer's other additions to this letter are part of the recurrent imagery of the poem as a whole, like the image of Criseyde as the lode star (V, 1392*) and the contrast between Criseyde's 'eyen clere' (V, 1338*) and Troilus's own:

> 'Myn eyen two, in veyn with which I se,
> Of sorwful teris salte arn woxen welles;'
>   (V, 1373–4*)

but even within this letter the phrase 'in veyn with which I se' may refer also to the intellectual blindness of Troilus. Criseyde's eyes are by contrast clear (as well as 'beautiful' or 'bright') – she has shown a clearsightedness in her final assessment of her own treachery (V, 1054–85*), as elsewhere in the poem,[24] which Troilus has never shared. But it is of no practical use to her, and in this respect their positions are the same as in the first two letters. Both this image and the following one of wells, which is paralleled by Troilus's reference to Criseyde as: 'of wele and wo my welle' (V, 1330*) (cf. I, 873* – 'of al my wo the welle') are also ironic, since they relate traditionally to the Virgin, whom Chaucer himself, in his *A.B.C.*, calls both: 'O verrey light of eyen that ben blynde' (*A.B.C.*, 105) and more conventionally, '. . . thiself, that art of pitee welle' (*A.B.C.*, 126).

Some other details added by Chaucer also tell against Criseyde; notable among them are the uses of the words *trewe* and *trouthe*. First, Troilus makes two simple references to his own fidelity (V, 1331–2,* V, 1365*). Then he connects the idea with Criseyde three times: 'yet thynketh on youre trouthe' (V, 1386*), where 'trouthe' is used in the narrow sense of a specific promise; '. . . myne owene deere herte trewe' (V, 1401*), which ironises Troilus's capacity for self-deception as well as Criseyde's treachery; and 'And to youre trouthe ay I me recomande' (V, 1414*), which could be taken to mean 'I am relying on your promise', or more ironically 'I commend myself to you (who are) true', or 'I am appealing to your inherent fidelity'. The last would also reflect on the way that Troilus trusts to the inherently fallible fidelity of a mortal woman, rather than the fidelity of God. This seems also to be glanced at by the Narrator's banal cliché:

> *Thus goth the world. God shilde us fro meschaunce,*
> *And every wight that meneth trouthe avaunce!*
> (V, 1434–5*)

Beneath the helpless shrug lies the imponderable problem of who, in this story, 'meneth trouthe'.

But Chaucer also introduces some details which more clearly imply limitations in Troilus himself, chiefly a heightening of the self-pity which he found in Troilo's letter:

> *'And if yow liketh knowen of the fare*
> *Of me, whos wo ther may no wit descryve,*
> *I kan namore but, chiste of every care,*
> *At wrytyng of this lettre I was on-lyve,*
> *Al redy out my woful gost to dryve;'*
> (V, 1366–70*)

One gets the impression that Troilus would have liked to have thought himself dead already if it had been possible. He also indulges in conventional paradox:

> 'My song, in pleynte of myn adversitee;
> My good, in harm; myn ese ek woxen helle is;'
> (and so on – V, 1375–6*)

This is reminiscent of Troilus's first song (I, 400–34*), and thus contrives the suggestion that he has not progressed at all since then.

Criseyde's final reply (V, 1590–1631*) has no single source. The structure of her letter is correct – a combined *salutatio* and *benevolentiae captatio* (V, 1590–6*); a *narratio*, relating her attitudes (V, 1597–1620*); a *peticio*, asking Troilus for friendship and not to be angered by her brevity (actually a virtue, according to pseudo-Alberich) (1621–6*); a second *benevolentiae captatio*, using *sententiae* (proverbs) – a method advocated by the anonymous Orleans *ars dictandi* (1627–30*); and a simple *conclusio* (1631*). The poise of her rhetoric is almost too perfect, and seems closer to the arts of poetry than to the more mundane skill of *dictamen*[25]– she opens, for example, with a fine apostrophe to Troilus (V, 1590–1*) of the kind which Geoffroi de Vinsauf calls *exclamatio*, used, as he recommends it, to express grief. She continues with a rhetorical question (*interrogacio*) (V, 1592–3*) and a beautiful combination of *determinatio* (the clarification of one part of speech by another) with rhetorical repetition, which Geoffroi calls *conduplicatio*: 'I herteles, I sik, I in destresse!' (V, 1594*).[26] The stanza is completed with a complicated antithesis (V, 1595–6*).

Criseyde's argument is equally contrived, balancing defensive and offensive arguments. Her defensive themes are:

1. An attempt to arouse his pity, partly by a rhetorical exposition of her unhappiness (e.g. V, 1592–4,* discussed above), and partly by a deliberate parade of fear (V, 1592,* 1603,* 1627* – the last two are somewhat less than convincing).
2. The promise to return to Troy when circumstances permit (V, 1601*, 1618–20*), undermined by the device of a syntactic break following an emphatic statement:

> 'Come I wole; but yet in swiche disjoynte
> I stonde as now, that what yer or what day
> That this shal be, that kan I naught apoynte.'
> (V, 1618–20*)

3. The pretence that their affair has been unimportant (V, 1606,* 1623–4*) and/or that its end has been inevitable (V, 1605*). This latter argument catches Troilus on a weak spot, for he has worked out the same excuse of predestination to relieve himself of responsibility (IV, 958–1078*).

Each of these leads to an accusation against Troilus:

1. The plea for pity is reinforced by the less than fair accusation that Troilus is thinking only of himself (V, 1607–8*).
2. The promise to return to Troy later is bolstered by the implication that she is being forced to allay suspicions about them because Troilus has failed to keep the affair secret (V, 1610–3*).
3. She alleges that she has heard that Troilus has only been trifling with her (V, 1614–5*), and although she then rejects this preposterous assertion, the fact that she voices it at all shows that she is prepared to make use of almost any argument. Her last two accusations (the totally false ones) both include the phrase 'beth nat wroth' (V, 1609,* 1614*), although elsewhere she has been quite capable of rebuking Troilus without apology when he deserved it (e.g. III, 1009–50*).

Some of her arguments conflict – if she is as miserable as the letter's fine opening suggests, how can their affair have been unimportant? If Troilus is justly accused of being preoccupied with his own misery, how can he have been trifling with her? The effect is to distance us from any involvement with her; we can now only guess at her real thoughts, without the commitment to them which is essential to an understanding of the earlier stages of the affair. This distancing is also inherent in the use of the letter form itself; we see the letter as received by Troilus, not as Criseyde is writing it (whereas we are shown Troilus writing his letter, V, 1303–16). It comes after she has made her farewell as a directly portrayed character, with her soliloquy (V, 1054–85*), which is more honest:

> 'For I have falsed oon the gentileste
> That evere was, and oon the worthieste!'
> (V, 1056–7*)

> 'And gilteles, I woot wel, I yow leve.
> But al shal passe; and thus take I my leve.'
> (V, 1084–5*)

The last phrase marks her real exit. Here she reappears only as an external facade, and her new remoteness forces us to consider her from a new viewpoint. There are poignant suggestions of an awareness behind the facade, like the constructive ambiguity[27] of: 'I herteles, I sik,' (V, 1594*) and of her last *sententia*: 'Th' entente is al, and nat the lettres space.' (V, 1630*). There are also echoes of earlier passages in the poem. The first two lines of the letter recall the idyllic song of Antigone in Book II (see especially II, 841–4*); her mention of the tears staining Troilus's letter (V, 1599–1600*) – real tears this time – remind one of Pandarus's play-acting advice just before Troilus's first letter: 'Biblotte it with thi teris ek a lite' (II, 1027*); and her excuse that she has heard rumours about herself and Troilus is drawn from the same passage of Ovid's *Heroides* (XVII, 149–51) as her protestation, just before her own reply to his first letter, that she has never written a letter before (II, 1213–14*).[28] But these ironies are not stressed, and neither we nor Troilus have any way of knowing whether or not she is still in love with him.

We need not assume that all the elements of the formal level will have the same main function in the poem, but this study has suggested that the letters are able, largely by virtue of their status as such, to provide a sensitive listener with a critical commentary on the narrated characters who are supposed to write them, without either endangering the sympathy of the audience for them or making the Narrator unduly perceptive or didactic. And this idea of a letter as a witness speaking for or against the writer can also be paralleled in medieval practice, as in the words of John Paston III, probably to his fiancée, Margery Brews:

> Her I send yow thys bylle wretyn wyth my lewd hand and sealyd wyth my sygnet to remayn wyth yow for a wyttnesse ayenst me, and to my shame and dyshonour if I contrary it.[29]

Chaucerian Comedy and Criseyde

ALFRED DAVID

What is love? 'tis not hereafter;
Present mirth hath present laughter;
What's to come is still unsure.
Twelfth Night, II. iii

Whatever else it may be, Chaucer is determined to make *Troilus and Criseyde* the tragedy of Troilus. He calls his book a 'tragedye' (V, 1786), and the plot does fulfil the definition of tragedy given by the Monk (*CT*. VII, 1973 ff.):[1] Troilus falls from the top of Fortune's wheel into the depths of misery and despair, driven finally to seek out his death on the battlefield.[2] However, no one regards the Monk's formula as adequate for *Troilus*. A poem in which the tragic hero's ghost is permitted to laugh at the mourners of his death obviously expresses a qualified view of the tragic experience. John Steadman has brilliantly traced the sources of this 'disembodied laughter' and shown how the philosophical and moral traditions behind it would deny the value of the earthly love and life that Troilus loses and, consequently, call into question our tragic sense of that loss.[3] To that extent, Troilus's celestial laughter is also at the expense of the reader's tragic sensibility.

Our final perspective on the tragedy of Troilus – that it is ultimately an exemplum of 'The blynde lust, the which that may nat laste' (V, 1824) – no longer brings with it the shock and disbelief that it used to create in many early modern readers of the poem. Criticism has gradually assimilated the ending and shown that it is, in fact, the only possible ending, foreshadowed from the very first through Chaucer's irony.[4] The student today is encouraged to look for irony everywhere in the poem, and there is certainly much ironic ambiguity if we see the story from a Boethian point of view, the long view that the scattered Boethian allusions encourage us to take. Seen in this way, the *Troilus* retains its wonderful doubleness yet still remains all of a piece, its contraries harmonized into a unified work of art.[5]

Satisfying as such a reading may be, it sacrifices, I believe, other aesthetic qualities in Chaucer's poem that are as wonderful as the sustained philosophical irony although they blur the unified vision and discord with the 'hevenyssh melodie' of the ending. We must not disregard another kind of laughter in the poem or confuse it with the ironic sort of which it is the antithesis. This kind of laughter is rarely ambiguous and not at all intellectual. For lack of a better term, I would call it 'bodily laughter' because, although it too laughs *at* the body, it does so out of sympathy in order to affirm, not to deny, the body's values.

The principal agent of bodily laughter in the poem is naturally Pandarus. Much of his clowning is on the subjects of food and sex. 'Nece', he replies to Criseyde's invitation to table, 'I have so gret a pyne / For love, that everich other day I faste' (II, 1165–6). The target of such jests is frequently the idealism of lovers like Troilus for whom food is a foe (I, 485), and particularly their conviction that love is a potentially fatal malady. Though, on the one hand, Pandarus's avowed purpose is to save his friend's life, on the other hand, he is constantly making jokes about Troilus's dying. 'Who is in his bed so soone / Iburied thus?' he asks, bringing Criseyde's letter to Troilus (II, 1310–11). 'God have thi soule, ibrought have I thi beere!' he whispers to Troilus, preparing him at the house of Deiphebus for Criseyde's entry (II, 1638).[6] This kind of humor expresses something more positive than ironic observations about the extravagance of lovers. It asserts through laughter the pleasures of eating, loving, and being alive. It is a form of humor Troilus does not understand at all, but it comes naturally to Criseyde. Pandarus makes Criseyde laugh so hard 'That she for laughter wende for to dye' (II, 1169). The expression 'to die of laughter' is only another way of saying what bodily laughter is all about, namely that the *last* thing we intend to do is to die.

Criseyde's whole nature is opposed to death and tragedy, and it is with her, not with Pandarus, whose credentials as a comic figure do not require restatement, that I am chiefly concerned. Chaucer has given her a sense of humor (completely absent in Boccaccio's heroine) that makes her the ideal audience for her uncle's japes and, in a more profound way, their innocent victim. When she and Pandarus are alone together they are constantly playing. Returning from her bedroom, where she has just read Troilus's love letter, she sneaks up behind Pandarus, pulls his hood, and exclaims in triumph: 'Ye were caught er that ye wiste' (II, 1182). Even such a light moment reveals her essential nature. Like Pandarus, Criseyde regards life as a most enjoyable game in which 'It nedeth me ful sleighly for to pleie' (II, 462).[7] She is well aware that she is the prize in a game Pandarus is playing, and she will let herself be won, so she believes, in her own time and on her own terms. She seeks fulfilment in love but not, like Troilus, apotheosis. Her struggle to survive and to preserve her precarious freedom in a world torn apart by the violent passions of men like Paris and Troilus constitutes another action within the main action of the poem that I should like to call the comedy of Criseyde. Unlike the tragedy of Troilus, the comic action has no ending, for Chaucer does not tell us what became of Criseyde. He left her story to be finished a century later by Robert Henryson, who turned it into another tragedy and transformed Criseyde's character. Henryson tells us how she was punished and how she died, but the comedy of Criseyde cannot end because the action of comedy is open-ended, the journey's end or lovers' meeting only a new beginning for the protagonists. In bidding farewell to his 'litel tragedye' Chaucer also prays that God may permit him 'to make in som comedye' (V, 1788). In writing those lines, Chaucer must have had some notion that a great deal of comedy already lay embedded in his tragedy of Troilus and that in the comic scenes he had found his truest vocation.[8]

The passage cited contains the only occurrence of the word *comedy* in Chaucer's writings, and his idea of comedy is obviously more vague than his idea of tragedy. Baugh in the excellent glossary to his edition does not list *tragedy* at all and glosses *comedye* for V, 1788, in the most general possible sense: 'cheerful poem or tale'.[9] Perhaps because Aristotle did not write a poetics of comedy, there has never been a theory of comedy as clearly defined as the theory of tragedy.[10] Nor have there been until quite recently any attempts to construct a systematic formal analysis of Chaucerian comedy comparable to Robertson's essay on tragedy.[11] The sheer variety of Chaucerian comedy seems to defy such endeavors, and Chaucer certainly never wrote comic tales by applying theoretical principles as he did in composing the Monk's tragedies.

To give a comprehensive definition of Chaucerian comedy, even if such a thing were possible, lies beyond the scope of this essay. Nevertheless, with the help of Fortune's wheel we can try to describe the comedy of Criseyde just as we can describe the tragedy of Troilus. There is of course the fact that just as one side of the wheel is descending, the other half is rising, as the Knight points out in criticizing the Monk's tragedies:

> And the contrarie is joye and greet solas,
> As whan a man hath been in povre estaat,
> And clymbeth up and wexeth fortunat,
> And there abideth in prosperitee.
> (*CT.* VII, 2774–7)

While this certainly shows the weakness of the Monk's idea of tragedy, it would be equally simplistic to take it as an idea of comedy.[12] According to the Boethian view, no man in this world can hope to abide in prosperity, and the only kind of comedy possible is divine comedy, which rises above worldly considerations. Robertson is right that medieval tragedy consists not in the mere accident of falling from Fortune's wheel but in an act of will by which one stakes one's ultimate happiness on Fortune.[13] The significant factor is not the direction in which the wheel is turning but the hero's disposition toward Fortune. The tragic hero is one who, like Troilus, expects the gifts of Fortune to be permanent and for whom the loss of those gifts is irretrievable. In contrast, the philosopher who disdains the transient gifts of Fortune places himself beyond human tragedy or comedy. But there is another type of character who refuses to be conquered by Fortune yet does not rise above her either. If he is thrown from her wheel, he seeks a way to rise again. Thus he continues to go round and round on Fortune's wheel, accepting and enjoying her gifts without despising them for their transience. For such a person none of life's joys or sorrows can ever be final so long as he remains on earth. Thus the movement of this kind of Chaucerian comedy is a going around in circles. The absurdity of the movement can inspire laughter or pity and often both responses at the same time. What chiefly distinguishes this kind of comedy is that it is sympathetic and not derisive or ironic. Seen *sub specie aeternitatis* the wrestling for this world may be laughable because the world is scorned. Seen *sub specie temporis*, however, the struggle is comic because the world is cherished.

Criseyde is just that type of character constantly going around in circles. The circular movement of Troilus's 'double sorwe', which makes one complete revolution of Fortune's wheel, as has been noted, provides the main action of the poem and gives it its tragic structure. Within this greater wheel, however, there is also the rapidly turning wheel of the 'aventures' of Criseyde, which are always changing 'fro wo to wele' and back again. The tale begins not with Troilus's first sorrow but with Criseyde's most recent calamity, her father's sudden departure for the Greek camp and the fuss being made about it by the irate populace.

Her appearance as a young widow, still in mourning, hints at earlier sorrow although we cannot tell how deeply she actually grieved for her late husband; her only explicit mention of her 'wedded lord' late in the poem (V, 974–76) is surely meant, and perhaps understood by Diomede to whom she makes it, as a veiled reference to Troilus. Boccaccio probably made his Criseida a widow because widows are supposed to be amorous. As Pandaro tells Troiolo: 'La mia cugina è vedova e disia' (II, 27).[14] Chaucer suppresses this line and emphasizes Criseyde's widowhood instead to command the reader's sympathy for her helpless and unprotected state. Boccaccio introduces his heroine with a simple statement about her difficulties and proceeds in the same sentence to describe her beauty:

> *Avea Calcàs lasciato in tanto male,*
> *sanza niente farlene sapere,*
> *una sua figlia vedova, la quale*
> *sì bella e sì angelica a vedere*
> *era . . .*
>
> (I, 11)

We are left to infer Criseida's feelings, but Chaucer expands this passage, spelling out Criseyde's fears, her bewilderment, her total isolation:

> *Now hadde Calkas left in this meschaunce,*
> *Al unwist of this false and wikked dede,*
> *His doughter, which that was in gret penaunce,*
> *For of hire lif she was ful sore in drede,*
> *As she that nyste what was best to rede;*
> *For bothe a widewe was she and allone*
> *Of any frend to whom she dorste hire mone.*
>
> (I, 92–8)

94

Apparently there is good reason to be afraid. Already in Boccaccio the majority of the people can scarcely be kept from setting fire to the house of Calchas, but Chaucer makes this even more dramatic, melodramatic in fact, making it appear as though the entire city were out to wreak vengeance by burning his innocent daughter:

> *and casten to be wroken*
> *On hym that falsly hadde his feith so broken,*
> *And seyden he and al his kyn at-ones*
> *Ben worthi for to brennen, fel and bones.*
>
> (I, 88–91)

Yet something about the *way* the Trojans in Chaucer express their united sense of outrage has a reassuringly comic effect. It may be partly overstatement, partly the homely ring of 'fel and bones' that makes Criseyde's situation seem like the imagined perils of romance from which she will be rescued by a good knight. Forty years ago it was still possible to regard such matters with total seriousness, as C. S. Lewis did in writing of Criseyde's 'pitiable longing, more childlike than womanly, for protection, for some strong stable thing that will hide her away and take the burden from her shoulders' and of Hector, 'whom she temporarily identifies with the strong defender of her dreams'.[15] A later generation has grown wary when Chaucer seems to be pulling out all the emotional stops. John Ganim aptly compares the picture of Criseyde on her knees before Hector to a late-medieval painting, so stylized that it keeps us emotionally at a safe distance. He also observes shrewdly that Criseyde's manner 'hirselven excusynge' (I, 112) is typical of her character although we can see this only with hindsight.[16] The scene is our first instance of the cycle of storm and calm in Criseyde's life. Hector dispels the threats against her with a noble speech, and after profuse thanks, she 'took hire leve, and hom, and held hir stille' (I, 126).

The opening scene hardly prepares us to meet Criseyde again at the beginning of the second book comfortably ensconced in 'wele', alongside two friends, being read to by a servant in a very well-appointed household; and yet I do not think many readers wonder at the change or ask where her trusted advisor, Uncle Pandarus, was keeping himself during the time of her troubles.[17] There is a sense, as we begin Book II, that Calchas and his treason are already as distant as 'kyng Layus' and 'Eddipus his sone' in the 'romaunce of Thebes' to which Criseyde and her friends are listening. Certainly there is irony in the fact that the inhabitants of one doomed city are so pleasurably being entertained by the tale of another doomed city, but as Pandarus arrives on this fine spring morning such considerations seem remote.

What immediately engages our interest is one of the most delightful comic scenes that Chaucer ever wrote. The comedy depends in large measure on our response to the tragic acting of Pandarus and Criseyde. In the case of Pandarus we can hardly miss it. Troilus's life, he tells her, lies in her hands, and so does his own:

> *'But if ye late hym deyen, I wol sterve –*
> *Have here my trouthe, nece, I nyl nat lyen –*
> *Al sholde I with this knyf my throte kerve.'*
> *With that the teris bruste out of his yen.*
>
> (II, 323–6)

The humor in Criseyde's case is not so easy to see because she is a woman and is behaving the way women under stress were once supposed to behave. Her first thought is, 'I shal felen what he meneth, ywis' (II, 387), and she noncommitally asks his advice. Pandarus's advice is *carpe diem*, and now it is her turn to burst into tears and call upon death:

> *'Allas, for wo! Why nere I deed?*
> *For of this world the feyth is al agoon. . . .*
>
> *'This false world, allas! Who may it leve?*
>
> *'What! is this al the joye and al the feste?*
> *Is this youre reed? Is this my blisful cas?*
> *Is this the verray mede of youre byheeste?*
> *Is al this paynted proces seyd, allas!*
> *Right for this fyn? O lady myn, Pallas!*
> *Thow in this dredful cas for me purveye,*
> *For so astoned am I that I deye.'*[18]
>
> (II, 409–10, 420–7)

Lewis comments on this performance: 'Few things in the poem are sadder or more illuminating than the burst of tears with which Criseyde receives the news, and the bitter reproach.'[19] But if we do not succumb to the stock response to a lady in distress, we might notice an amusing discrepancy between the elevated style of her outburst and the facts of this 'dredful cas'. The fear Lewis regards as the mainspring of Criseyde's character may be real enough, but it is easily aroused and easily allayed. Criseyde always reacts in the same way when she is upset, whether an angry mob seems to be threatening her life or her uncle not paying proper regard to her honor.

Moreover, there is humor in the way Pandarus and Criseyde vie with one another in expressing injury and indignation, a contest in which he is more than a match for her:

> '*O cruel god, O dispitouse Marte,*
> *O Furies thre of helle, on yow I crye!* . . .
>
> '*But sith it liketh yow that I be ded,*
> *By Neptunus, that god is of the see,*
> *Fro this forth shal I nevere eten bred*
> *Til I myn owen herte blood may see;*
> *For certeyn I wol deye as soone as he.*'
>
> (II, 435–46)

Pandarus manages to half-convince Criseyde (possibly even himself) that he might try something desperate, but the reader cannot take him seriously, and neither need we take Criseyde's protestations at face value. The oaths, the threats, the tears are all part of the game. Pandarus's eloquence is partly meant as a compliment to Criseyde's honor, and her 'Daunger' must be a worthy challenge to his art of persuasion. Neither partner must take the other one for granted. At one point, when Pandarus lets his match-making imagination rush too far ahead, Criseyde corrects him as one might catch one's opponent playing out of turn:

> '*Nay, therof spak I nought, ha, ha!*' *quod she,*
> '*As helpe me God, ye shenden every deel!*'
>
> (II, 589–90)

The comedy turns on the difference in style and tone between Criseyde's 'Allas!' and her 'ha, ha!'.

I am not accusing either Criseyde or Pandarus of insincerity – at least not in this scene. The tears and tempestuous emotions are all genuine enough. If they had to be fabricated, as Diomede for example fabricates the sentiments he professes to feel for Criseyde immediately after he has first met her (V, 106–75), the scene would be satire instead of comedy. The comedy lies precisely in the fact that Pandarus and Criseyde can mount so high on wings of fantasy and come down again as quickly to ordinary speech and practical affairs. In the emotional ups and downs of Criseyde's day we can see the comic epitome of what happens when fortune turns her wheel.

Fortune is the subject of the talk between uncle and niece. Both think and speak about Troilus's love as *her* Fortune – 'aventure', 'chaunce', or 'cas' – an extraordinary piece of good luck from his point of view, another ill chance from hers. Pandarus presents himself as the messenger of good Fortune: 'to every wight some goodly aventure / Som tyme is shape' (II, 281–2). Criseyde feels that Fortune has presented her with a new dilemma: 'A! Lord! what me is tid a sory chaunce! / For myn estat lith now in jupartie' (II, 464–5). Yet, as always, she resigns herself to making the best of a bad situation:

> '*But natheles, with Goddes governaunce,*
> *I shal so doon, myn honour shal I kepe,*
> *And ek his lif,*' *– and stynte for to wepe.*
>
> (II, 467–9)

In the brief time since Pandarus paid his call, she has passed from laughter to tears, and soon this latest crisis is put behind: 'Tho fillen they in other tales glade' (II, 498). Within this framework, the weeping, the talk of death and of this false world proves ephemeral and unreal. Now that the storm has passed over, it is Criseyde who steers the conversation back to Troilus, inquiring with evident curiosity (and incidentally teasing Pandarus a little): 'Tel me how first ye wisten of his wo. / Woot noon of it but ye? . . . Kan he wel speke of love?' (II, 501–3). No wonder that when Pandarus leaves at last, 'Lord, so he was glad' (II, 597), and the reader, if he can for the moment forget Boethius, can be glad too.

The same pattern repeats itself through the balance of Book II and the first half of Book III. There is Pandarus's made-up story about the dastardly Poliphete and his nefarious plot to bring legal action against Criseyde (II, 1464–84), the occasion for the dinner at the house of Deiphebus. Criseyde turns pale at the news and moans, 'What shal I doon, allas?' (II, 1472). There is the story concocted about Troilus's jealousy of Horaste at which she exclaims: 'Allas! conceytes wronge, / What harm they don, for now lyve I to longe!' (III, 804–5). We may think Criseyde pathetically trusting, or we may think her somewhat gullible like a character in a fabliau. Pandarus certainly knows his niece well enough to exploit her instinctive fears; perhaps he also understands that the crises he invents fulfil an emotional need for Criseyde and that she *wants* to be deceived. She cannot yield to Troilus except in the course of some high drama in which she is the innocent victim of false accusations, and so Pandarus contrives his incredibly complicated comedy not from any practical

98

necessity but to satisfy the demands of Criseyde's romantic
tion of herself.

In all of these episodes, Chaucer makes us accomp
Pandarus's conspiracy to bring the lovers together. In a Boethian
sense, the reader is privileged to watch the intrigue from a providen-
tial point of view while Criseyde has only the limited perspective of
Fortune. 'God and Pandare wist al what this mente' (II, 1561),
comments Chaucer as the guests assemble at the house of Deiphebus.
We know t[...]d therefore we can smile at the trials and tears of
Criseyde as [...]elf yet also
with her u[...]the course
of true love [...]oth. Up to
this point [...]s romantic
comedies, [...]s romantic
comedies read like the most [...], for I am
convinced Shakespeare learned more about comedy from Chaucer
than from any other author. There is, of course, more to *Troilus* than
this. I am not forgetting the ending or the irony. I would say,
however, that through the middle of Book III, Chaucerian comedy
makes light of the hereafter. Seen in the perspective of the ending, the
moral of Criseyde's little Boethian speech on false felicity – 'Ther is
no verray weele in this world heere' (III, 836) – is an ironic comment
on the love scene that follows. Seen in the context of the third book,
the love scene makes fun not only of Criseyde's sententiousness but of
the moral itself. Boethius like the melancholy Jacques is made part of
the comedy to gladden our hearts.

For Troilus, the fourth book brings about the peripeteia; his
tragedy commences. But the comedy of Criseyde continues even
though the joy has gone out of it. The sadness of the final books does
not turn comedy into something else but rather forces us to accept the
implications of a comic view of life and deepens our sense of the
meaning of comedy. Great comedy is edged with sadness. The same
characteristics in Criseyde that delighted us before – her sense of
drama, her fair welcome and her reserve, her desire above all else to
please and to avoid blame – become painful now that she is struggling
in the grip of real misfortune. But her character enables her to survive
the separation while Troilus is destroyed by it.

The episodes of the fourth book repeat those of the earlier books:
Troilus suffers in his bedroom, Pandarus shuttles back and forth with
messages and advice, Criseyde 'After the deth she cryed a thousand
sithe' (IV, 753). The wheels continue to go round. Criseyde's tears

and grief are more intense and genuinely pitiable, but as always her tragedy is consummated chiefly in the imagination, leaving her free to make the best of things. Like Boccaccio's heroine (IV, 89), Criseyde vows that she will starve herself to death, but Chaucer adds a touch:

> I shal doon thus, syn neither swerd ne darte
> Dar I noon handle, for the crueltee . . .
>
> (IV, 771–2)

Even without this mention of her aversion to cold steel, we know that Criseyde is no Juliet, and we cannot believe her when she tells Troilus that if he had killed himself, she, too, would have slain herself with his sword. Her true feelings about suicide are expressed in her first reaction when Troilus tells her why the bare sword is lying there: 'O mercy, God, lo, which a dede!' (IV, 1231). There is a note of incredulity when she asks, as though to make sure that she has heard correctly, a second time (another addition to the scene by Chaucer):

> 'Than if I nadde spoken, as grace was,
> Ye wolde han slayn youreself anon?'
>
> (IV, 1233–4)

It is only in response to his matter of fact 'Yee, douteles', that she assumes the grand style of tragedy:

> 'Allas!
> For, by that ilke Lord that made me,
> I nolde a forlong wey on lyve have be,
> After youre deth, to han ben crowned queene
> Of al the lond the sonne on shyneth sheene.
>
> 'But with this selve swerd, which that here is,
> Myselve I wolde han slawe.'
>
> (IV, 1235–41)

She believes that she would have done it just as she believes the many reasons she gives Troilus why he can be sure that she will return to him. She can believe it because she is protected against the truth by her inability to see the future. She knows this much about herself and says so when she is regretting that she did not run off with Troilus:

100

> *'Prudence, allas, oon of thyne eyen thre*
> *Me lakked alwey, er that I come here!*
> *On tyme ypassed wel remembred me,*
> *And present tyme ek koud ich wel ise,*
> *But future tyme, er I was in the snare,*
> *Koude I nat sen; that causeth now my care.'*
>
> (V, 744–9)

And she immediately proceeds to prove the truth of that assertion by declaring:

> *'But natheles, bityde what bityde,*
> *I shal to-morwe at nyght, by est or west,*
> *Out of this oost stele on som manere syde,*
> *And gon with Troilus where as hym lest.*
> *This purpos wol ich holde, and this is best.'*
>
> (V, 750–4)

Saying what she will do tomorrow is Criseyde's standard way of dealing with a difficult situation. 'So shal I do to-morwe, ywys' (III, 848), she tells Pandarus when he asks her to speak to Troilus about his jealousy, and to Diomede she will say, 'To-morwe ek wol I speken with yow fayn, / So that ye touchen naught of this matere' (V, 995–6). Criseyde lives in the past and the present, and when things go wrong there is always a new day fraught with possibilities to redeem the lost time. Criseyde is the direct opposite of the tragic heroine Cassandra who is able to see the future but is impotent to do anything about it. Criseyde cannot see the future but believes she can always do something about it. And, in a way, there is always something to be done although it may not be what she first contemplated doing.

There is Diomede. Once again Criseyde is in mourning when she meets him, and she repels his advances in her characteristic manner:

> *'Ek, God woot, love and I ben fer ysonder!*
> *I am disposed bet, so mot I go,*
> *Unto my deth, to pleyne and maken wo.'*
>
> (V, 983–5)

But there is a kind of promise in the denial: 'What I shal after don, I kan nat seye' (986). The reader can say, however, and should be able to say even if he had not been told in a dozen different ways of the ending. The notion that Criseyde's character changes – that Chaucer has violated the consistency of her character because the plot demanded it – could arise only through a wilful misunderstanding of her character. In one sense Criseyde is constantly changing in the poem, but in a deeper sense she never changes because she is constant in her mutability. The one thing that is sure is that she will get over her present sorrow to encounter future ones, and those, too, will pass by. Nor will her tomorrows creep by in any petty pace, but they will be filled with drama and excitement. Life with Diomede brings its crises, and when he is wounded by Troilus, we learn, 'tho wepte she many a teere, / Whan that she saugh his wyde wowndes blede' (V, 1046–7). Her portrait is drawn accurately:

> *Ne nevere mo ne lakked hire pite;*
> *Tendre-herted, slydynge of corage.*
> (V, 824–5)

During the earlier part of this century, critics were fascinated by the character of Criseyde and there were widely differing interpretations of it. I have had occasion to discuss C. S. Lewis's sentimental conception of her 'ruling passion' as 'Fear'.[20] R. K. Root turns her into Coleridge's Hamlet: 'Chaucer's heroine, with all her beauty and womanly loveliness and grace of demeanor, has from the beginning of the story a fatal weakness – the inability to make a deliberate choice. She thinks always too precisely on the event'.[21] In the criticism, at least, the heroine of the *Troilus* quite stole the stage from the hero. One of the achievements of more recent criticism has been to go beyond this Bradleyan approach to Chaucer's poem and to restore Troilus to his rightful place as the central character in a *medieval*, as opposed to an ancient or Renaissance, tragedy.

Another consequence of the re-evaluation of the poem has been the recognition of the symbolic dimension of Chaucer's characters. Because Criseyde is caught up in the cyclical process of the world, critics have seen her mutability as a symbol of change, the human equivalent, as it were, of Lady Fortune or Dame Nature. While there is undoubtedly justification for looking at her in this larger sense, there is danger of losing the woman in the symbol. There is also danger of losing the comedy. Though we may personify Fortune or Nature, they remain abstractions who do not respond from specific motives to particular situations. Chaucer has invested a great deal of art not only in individualizing Boccaccio's stereotyped heroine but in creating the circumstances that reveal her character and help to account for her actions. Perhaps he did his work too well. The older critics were, I believe, right in regarding the character of Criseyde as his finest achievement in the poem even though they were not always just to the character of Troilus or to the moral and philosophical import that Chaucer took such pains to introduce into the story of the two lovers.

We cannot dispose of Criseyde as the incarnation of the forces that brought about the downfall of Troilus. Her presence in the poem is too powerful for that. She is a comic creation of such vitality that it challenges the idea of tragedy and the authority of the advice that bids us to repair 'hom fro worldly vanyte' (V, 1837). Criseyde's message is rather that our home is here on 'This litel spot of erthe' (V, 1815) to have and to hold while there is time.

In his poem, Chaucer leaves Criseyde to history and to heaven:

> *Ne me ne list this sely womman chyde*
> *Forther than the storye wol devyse.*
> *Hire name, allas! is punysshed so wide,*
> *That for hire gilt it oughte ynough suffise.*
> (V, 1093–6)

We know about her earthly fame, but what about the heavenly? Troilus goes forth to dwell among the stars and has his reward, whatever or wherever that may be. What of Criseyde? Ostensibly out of 'routhe', Chaucer chooses to beg that question. A century later his disciple Henryson set out to answer it in the *Testament of Cresseid*, which is much more like a medieval tragedy than is Chaucer's *Troilus*. He tells us that Criseyde did fall: she is cast off by Diomede, becomes a common prostitute, and is afflicted with leprosy. Excessive as such punishment may seem to a modern reader, from a medieval and Christian point of view, Henryson has been kinder to Criseyde than Chaucer, for in his poem she is brought finally to confess her sins and we may be quite certain that his Cresseid ends well in the only way that is supposed to matter.

Chaucer chose a different direction. After *Troilus* he never again tells us about the final destination of his characters. Concerning Arcite he says only,

> *His spirit chaunged hous and wente ther,*
> *As I cam nevere, I kan nat tellen wher.*
> *Therfore I stynte, I nam no divinistre.*
> (*CT.* I, 2809–11)

Possibly Chaucer (or the Knight) cannot say because the stanzas from the *Teseida* describing the flight of Arcite's soul to the eighth

103

sphere had already been used for Troilus, but Chaucer did not really have to raise the question in the Knight's Tale. It sounds very much as though Chaucer had come to prefer writing about men's mortal bodies instead of about their immortal souls. The *Canterbury Tales* is, in any case, not the sort of work that lends itself to predicting the final destinations of the pilgrims although some contemporary critics have not been slow to pronounce such judgements.

It is in the *Canterbury Tales* that I think we must look for a worthy continuation of the Chaucerian comedy represented by Criseyde. We find it, I believe, in the Wife of Bath's Prologue and Tale. Superficially the Wife has little in common with Criseyde. She is not in the least gentle, fearful, or tender-hearted. She is aggressively and boisterously lower-middle-class. Yet, if we disregard such superficialities, I believe we may find that Criseyde and Alisoun are sisters and share the really essential things. Both are widows careful of their 'estat' and 'purveiaunce'. Both consider themselves to be exceedingly practical women though both are at bottom hopelessly romantic. Both have been through good times and bad, and their experience has made them somewhat sententious and skeptical, yet both remain firmly committed to life. They are comic heroines who go round and round on Fortune's wheel and who believe in the future, beating against the current even as they are borne back ceaselessly into the past. 'But yet to be right myrie wol I fonde', says the Wife of Bath (*CT*. III, 479). 'To Diomede algate I wol be trewe', says Criseyde (V, 1071). It comes to much the same thing.

Troilus, Books I–III: A Criseydan Reading

MARK LAMBERT

As its opening lines announce, Chaucer's poem is about the adventures of Prince Troilus. He is our representative in the work, the human being seeking happiness, just as you and I do, in sublunary things. And Criseyde, the charming, faithless heroine, is the good of this world, that which the hero seeks, finds, and must inevitably lose. In Chaucer's narrative statement, Troilus is the subject, Criseyde the object. Most readers of *Troilus and Criseyde* will, I think, agree on this much, and I say their opinion is good. But Chaucer's *Troilus* (and about this too I hope most of us will agree) is not only an extraordinarily rich, but a strangely shifting, shimmering work, and whatever things we say about it, we soon find ourselves adding 'yes, but . . .' The present essay is just such a 'yes, but' qualification. What I want to argue before parting from you is that in the first half of Chaucer's poem, that is from the opening through the end of Book III, the reader's experience is in fact more interestingly like Criseyde's than like Troilus's. It is not that I wish to justify the heroine's actions; what I want to present, rather, is a Criseydan reading of the sorrow of Troilus, a tracing of affinities between her sensibility and our sense of the work of which she's part.

Now of course there are few statements to be made about Criseyde's sensibility that will not themselves bring forth a throng of 'yes, but' qualifications: it is in good part because the reader must keep reinterpreting her that the entire poem shimmers as it does. What concerns me here is not any key to the whole character of Criseyde, but rather the thing about her which is most stressed as we experience the early books: she is timid, she is cautious. In *The Allegory of Love*, C. S. Lewis took fear to be Criseyde's ruling passion;[1] not being quite easy with the idea of a ruling passion here, I'd rather say that fear is the dominant color in the initial portrait, or a clear tone sounded early, and never forgotten.

We start, then, with a markedly timid heroine. And one thing this easily frightened lady understands to be frequently true is something we, Chaucer's audience, know will be true in the present case: love brings suffering. We are reading a poem about the double sorrow of Troilus; the heroine believes love is 'the mooste stormy lyf, / Right of hymself, that evere was bigonne' (II, 778–9).[2] In moving through the first half of the narrative, both heroine and reader are soothed into hopefulness. Criseyde is made to overcome her timidity and worst suspicions, we to put aside our foreknowledge. The first hemisphere of the *Troilus* is a great poem of seduction.

The seduction of Criseyde is not, most significantly, an eroticizing but an heroicizing of her life. I have been referring to her as the poem's heroine, but this, after all, is not quite an appropriate term for Criseyde. That timidity has presumably led to, and in any case is usually accompanied by, a certain modesty of aspiration; like a Chaucerian narrator, she is someone who would rather not be carried about by eagles. Criseyde remains quietly within the bounds of the ordinary and expected, abiding, Chaucer tells us at the end of the brief episode in which she is introduced, 'with swich meyne / As til hire honour nede was to holde' (I, 127–8). Though herself a creature of superlative beauty, Criseyde has no taste for the extreme, little interest in any light beyond the light of common day. The *gods* of Love, endlessly invoked and referred to by others, are not named at all by Criseyde until fairly late in the fourth book.

For Criseyde the primary question is not, to what height of bliss? but, is this going to hurt? Thus, when she has her eagle dream, what is wonderful is the lack of pain:

> *And as she slep, anonright tho hire mette*
> *How that an egle, fethered whit as bon,*
> *Undir hire brest his longe clawes sette,*
> *And out hire herte he rente, and that anon,*
> *And dide his herte into hire brest to gon,*
> *Of which she nought agroos, ne nothyng smerte;*
> *And forth he fleigh, with herte left for herte.*
> (II, 925–31)

Not as snow or a lily, but white as *bon*: ivory, but the overtones are unpleasant. Criseyde needs to be reassured about terrible beauty, coaxed into joining the company of Gottfried's noble hearts and Yeats's tragic heroines.[3]

Finally, though, one can't quite be soothed into heroism; at best one can be convinced that although the price is high, it is worth paying. Criseyde, however, must be led to believe that the price is really no price at all: love isn't going to hurt one bit. The *Cantus Antigone*, that effective persuader, touches lightly on the truth of love as a heroic experience: 'No wele is worth, that may no sorwe dryen' (II, 866); love, scorned by wretches, is like the bright sun, which a man may not look at directly 'for feeblesse of his yen' (863). But Antigone's song is basically a case-history, and that history is of life led 'in alle joie and seurte' (833). It will seem to Chaucer's heroine that the important danger is on the other side, and frightful things may happen if she is unresponsive.

Now Criseyde as I have described her thus far should be recognizable to readers of Chaucer's poem and only too familiar to readers of Chaucer criticism: a low, trembling, unworthy thing, this Criseyde. True enough; but there is indeed a positive to this negative, and that positive, I shall say with heroic boldness, is the source of our main pleasure as we read through the early books of this narrative. In these books we have the poetry of just such a life as this Criseyde would find comfortable; the poetry of Chaucerian Trojanness, of the kindly, the endearing, the contained. To experience the first half of the *Troilus* is to be charmed by the unheroic.

This poetry of the unheroic (about which I shall be saying more in a moment) brings us close to Criseyde. What is still more interesting, though, is that way in which we, like Chaucer's timid widow, are seduced into forgetting the limitations of the quiet life – or, to put this more precisely, into overlooking the special demands of the heroic. Much as we know from the beginning of the work that Troy is doomed, and yet come to believe, while reading along from stanza to stanza, that somehow that Greek siege hasn't *really* changed things—

> But though that Grekes hem of Troie shetten,
> And hire cite biseged al aboute,
> Hire olde usage nolde they nat letten,
> As for to honoure hir goddes ful devoute . . .
>
> (I, 148–51)

—so we put aside our knowledge of what love is, and come to believe, as Criseyde herself does, that there can be snugness amid hyperboles.

One may be easy in the presence of grand gestures. The heroic is manageable, and, in fact, a hero's passion, rightly considered, may be quite a convenient thing. Of this Criseyde, with some help from Pandarus, convinces herself. More insidiously, Chaucer teaches a similar lesson to the reader by the manner in which he presents his hero. Consider Troilus, for a moment, not as either a psychological study or an Everyman, but as a representative of the Heroic. He is a fierce warrior, the second greatest in the city. He is very eager to strike tragic attitudes – those attitudes which will finally prove to be the appropriate ones. Troilus wants to understand clearly, and asks difficult questions: Boethian ones later, Petrarchan ones here. He laughs very little, and what humor he does have is of a markedly sardonic kind.[4] He deals in life and death: when he needs something to keep his brother and sister-in-law out of the room for a while, he luckily finds to hand a letter from Hector asking whether a certain man should be allowed to live or not.

Described in this way, Troilus seems fully qualified to represent the Other, Criseyde's opposite. Less schematically regarded, this Troilus sounds like just the kind of suitor to frighten Criseyde out of her wits. But of course Chaucer's protagonist isn't *really* like that, doesn't seem a huge or forbidding presence, even though all the things I have mentioned are there in the text. Just so: it is the distance between our usual reaction to such characteristics and our response to Troilus in the early books of this poem which is the measure of Chaucer's artfulness, his domestication of heroic intensity.

Chaucer's Troilus is a sort of *trompe l'œil* performance; the heroism is rendered, but camouflaged by a peculiar background and the artist's cunning selection of an odd angle of vision. Troilus's war-making is extramural, and not seen in detail. His behavior is impeccably heroic; but it is just here, when one is in love, that proper heroic behavior is largely a matter of going to bed and moaning with some frequency, and it is just this kind of heroic behavior that Chaucer puts in sharp focus. Troilus is a hyperbolist: whatsoever his hand finds to do, he does with his might. He is, as Pandarus sees, one of the great heretics who, when converted, become great champions of the faith. But, in the first half of the poem, Troilus seems the most comically ineffective of the characters we observe. Those large gestures of his are absurdly out of place. He has never noticed that this world he inhabits is manageable, providing more employment for good-natured engineers than for Titans. And if our heroine, Criseyde,

is not of Troilian intenseness, well, isn't that intenseness really a kind of silliness? Surely she is more than a match for this young man: the qualities she lacks and he possesses seem ridiculous encumbrances.

Chaucer's hero does some slightly foolish things, but the main reason he appears silly is that we see him within Chaucer's Troy. It is an extraordinary setting. This fourteenth-century Troy is, it seems to me, one of the great *città invisibili* of English literature, one of the wonderful places of our imaginations. What meanness there is here exists only to summon forth its opposite. Chaucerian Troy is the city of kindliness and friendship, and, at least for the post-Romantic reader – at least but perhaps inevitably for the post-Romantic reader – a town of childhood. Like Troilus's martial deeds, parents are absent or glimpsed in the distance; they are never directly quoted in this great poem of talk. (The exception here, the one substantial parent, is Calchas, and the narrative begins with his departure from the city.) In this Troy it is Pandarus who stands *in loco parentis*, and he is our remembered ideal uncle: all the competence of a father and none of the authority; half a peer, half an elder. (Thus the familiar question: how old are we to suppose Pandarus to be?) Nor is it only parents who are kept out of the way. No wives, husbands or lovers appear with their partners except for the hero and heroine themselves: Helen's Paris and Pandarus's lady are mere *data*. Sexual pairing, stern and venerable authority, the risking and taking of life, are things referred to, but not carefully observed. The clearly seen, directly audible world is populated, as we shall see, by people for whom friendliness is the principal emotion, people who seem to like simply being in one another's company.

Late in the work, Troilus speaks about things he fears may happen if Criseyde does leave the city of Troy and go to the enemy camp. Among the Greeks she'll find so many worthy knights doing their utmost to please her,

> '. . . That ye shul dullen of the rudenesse
> Of us sely Troians, but if routhe
> Remorde yow, or vertu of youre trouthe . . .'
> (IV, 1489–91)

'The rudenesse of us sely Troians': it is in one sense a new idea about Troy, but when we come upon these lines they somehow seem right, the fear they express not unreasonable. Troilus's anxiety echoes something in our experience of the poem. Troy (and when considered as part of it, even the heroic Troilus) is not truly of the great world,

109

but remains innocent, sheltered, *sely*. The feared Greeks, to whom the heroine's father goes as the story begins, and who will be moved to pity by the plea of 'this olde greye' for the restoration of his daughter (IV, 64–133), are the grown-ups of *Troilus and Criseyde*.[5]

The *Troilus* is a poem about love, but it is set in Troy, which is supremely the city of friendship. The first books of the narrative do with the overwhelming experience of love what they do with the fierce warrior Troilus: not deny, nor even fail to mention, all that is high, and solitary and most stern (Chaucer's stanzas of commentary certainly tell of the uniqueness and power of Eros)[6] but emphasize what is comfortable. Here Chaucer plays to his own ends with the truisms, rhetorical habits, and philosophical interests of his age. What is friendship? What is love? How are they alike? How do they differ? As Gervase Mathew says of Anglo-Norman literature, 'it is notoriously difficult to distinguish between advice to friends and advice to lovers at a time when love between man and woman was expressed in terms of friendship, and friendship between man and man was expressed in terms of love'.[7] This is the kind of situation our poet loves, and one of the most delightfully vertiginous things in Chaucer's narrative is the way Pandarus and the author juggle and whisk around various ideas about love's relation to friendship. One may ask for the friendliness of a loved lady; one uses 'love of frendshipe' as a disguise for a love which is not friendship; but then, 'love of frendshipe' may be a stage in a progress toward a move not of friendship, etc. Pandarus plays more conspicuously with the categories, Chaucer with the textures of the two experiences.

The ecstasy of love is not to be described in words, no more than is the joy of heaven. But stanza by stanza, as I say, the narrative presence of love is something manageable, a special form of friendliness. Let's turn again to the scene in which Criseyde is introduced. There, we will remember, what she needs is the friendship Chaucerian Troy can so well supply. She is

> *in gret penaunce,*
> *For of hir lif she was ful sore in drede,*
> *As she that nyste what was best to rede;*
> *For bothe a widewe was she and allone*
> *Of any frend to whom she dorste hir mone.*
>
> (I, 94–8)

Initially she is observed as a disconsolate seeker of friendship; before long, Troilus is presented as a disconsolate seeker of love. We start with the two needs as parallel, and Chaucer goes on to interweave the two emotions. The gestures of love are also the gestures of kindliness. On the night of the smoky rain, when Troilus, brought to his lady's bed and afraid that she is angry with him, kneels before her and pleads, 'God woot that of this game, / Whan al is wist, than am I nought to blame' (III, 1084–5), he is much like the friendless Criseyde who had knelt before Hector and excused herself. Though Troilus faints here and Criseyde did not in the earlier scene, the two emotions seem to be of like intensity: the lover of Book III 'felte he nas but deed' (III, 1081), the widow was well nigh out of her wit with sorrow and fear. In a work where a lovelorn character sounds much like a friendlorn character, the reader does not find it easy to keep the uniqueness of love steadily in view. Structure joins what doctrinal passages put asunder.

A more amusing example of the assimilation of love and friendship comes from the stanzas in which Pandarus is introduced. We have here, one need hardly say, a wonderful entrance scene. Pandarus is the narrative's great expediter, almost Human Resourcefulness itself. Appropriately, we first meet him as he bursts into a room where he is needed. Notice, though, that there has in fact been some interesting verbal preparation for his entrance. A few lines before Pandarus appears, we hear the last words quoted in direct discourse from Troilus's complaint to his absent lady: '. . . And with som *frendly* lok gladeth me, swete, / Though nevere more thing ye me byheete' (I, 538–9). Apparently one part of the hero's prayer is granted, the other carried off on the winds. Troilus is shown the friendliness he wants – but not by Criseyde:

> *Bywayling in his chambre thus allone,*
> *A frend of his, that called was Pandare,*
> *Com oones in unwar, and herde hym groone,*
> *And say his frend in swich destresse and care.*
>
> (I, 547–50)

Some eighty lines earlier Troilus had wished for his lady's compassion:

> '. . . *now wolde God, Criseyde,*
> *Ye wolden on me rewe, er that I deyde!*
> *My dere herte, allas! myn hele and hewe*
> *And lif is lost, but ye wol on me rewe'.*
>
> (I, 459–62)

111

Now we hear:

> *This Pandare, that neigh malt for wo and routhe,*
> *Ful ofte seyde, 'Allas! what may this be?*
> *Now frend', quod he, 'if evere love or trouthe*
> *Hath ben, or is, bitwixen the and me,*
> *Ne do thow nevere swich a crueltee*
> *To hiden fro thi frend so gret a care! . . .'*
>
> (I, 582–7)

Thus Chaucer gives us Pandarus, the poem's supreme blurrer of love and friendship.

My friend's fortune in love is my fortune also: Pandarus's repeated *us* to refer to himself and Troilus as a pair whose happiness depends upon the kindness of his niece (a usage which has pushed up a fair number of eyebrows among our contemporaries) is much to the point here. That amiable *we* is perhaps most interesting when Pandarus assures Criseyde that Troilus's death for love will entail his own death for friendship. Consider the effects of this asseveration upon both the heroine and ourselves. Criseyde has heard about tragic, hyperbolic love:

> *'Unhappes fallen thikke*
> *Alday for love, and in swych manere cas*
> *As men ben cruel in hemself and wikke . . .'*
>
> (II, 456–8)

She apparently goes on to accept the possibility of *Freundschaftestod* as well (II, 459–60). Seeing she must play 'ful sleighly', Criseyde immediately and successfully does so. Negotiations are conducted, and by the end of the scene there is no imminent danger of death for love, death for friendship, or scandal. What Criseyde has learned here, really, is that the universe of high emotions and death for grief has denizens as familiar as her uncle Pandarus – and she certainly knows how to deal with *him*. When people get up to leave, saying things like

> *' . . . But sith it liketh yow that I be ded,*
> *By Neptunus, that god is of the see,*
> *Fro this forth shal I nevere eten bred*
> *Til I myn owen herte blood may see;*
> *For certeyn I wol deye as soone as he'*
>
> (II, 442–6)

one can still control matters with the familiar gestures of a less operatic world. The stanza ends, charmingly, 'And up he sterte, and on his wey he raughte, / Til she agayn hym by the lappe kaughte'.[8]

Thus, by association, heroic love comes to seem familiar and manageable. In this case it is *perhaps* by Pandarian design that this impression is created, but elsewhere in the poem the domestication of the heroic for reader and heroine is of a sort beyond the powers of even the cleverest uncle. A nice instance here involves that dream of the eagle I spoke of a few pages ago. In itself, of course, that vision was reassuring – there was no pain in that exchange of hearts – but the reassurance was of a negative kind. Fortunate, then, that some two hundred lines later in the second book Pandarus unwittingly parodies and domesticates – Trojanizes – the eagle's gesture. Criseyde does not want to accept the letter her uncle has brought from Troilus, and so Pandarus, Chaucer tells us, 'hente hire faste, / And in hire bosom the lettre down he thraste . . .' (II, 1154–5). (In Chaucer's English *bosom* can mean either the breast or the part of a robe covering the breast: a useful doubleness here.) The rapture of love now comes to seem rather like being seized by uncle Pandarus: familiar and out-maneuverable uncle Pandarus. He

> *seyde hire, 'Now cast it awey anon,*
> *That folk may seen and gauren on us tweye'.*
> *Quod she, 'I kan abyde til they be gon';*
> *And gan to smyle . . .*
>
> (II, 1156–9)

And, reader, we smile with her. Thirty lines later, Criseyde finds that this man who thought he could trap her is himself quite trappable: returning from her reading of the letter, she takes Pandarus by the hood as he stands in a study. *She* is the one who can say, 'Ye were caught er that ye wiste' (II, 1182). This, in turn, is a statement we ought to recall when we hear her lover say to Criseyde, 'Now be ye kaught . . . now yeldeth yow . . .' (III, 1207–8).

Criseyde's uncle not only domesticates love but is himself love domesticated. Again: we are often unsure just where his manipulation ends and that of a larger, vaguer force begins, but if we wish to resist the poem's seductive blurring and try to sort things out, we may assume that Pandarus knows his niece will be affected by a reminder that he, her familiar *em*, is that strange creature, a lover. Out of such awareness, or 'by aventure, or sort, or cas', Pandarus does bring the running joke of his own unhappy love into the openings of both his early embassies to Criseyde. But, whether he is being artful at these moments or not, it is clear that Pandarus's love service is real, a fact of the narrative and not merely a ploy. And *this* means, if one thinks about it, that the Pandarian version of love works upon the reader much as it does upon the heroine: quick death fades into that less horrific oxymoron, jolly woe. The sort of effect I have in mind here is perhaps most noticeable in the Pandarus-and-the-swallow stanzas which open the action of Book II. The friend and uncle is about to set off for the first of his visits to Criseyde. But it is May now, and so it happens

> *That Pandarus, for al his wise speche,*
> *Felt ek his part of loves shotes keene,*
> *That, koude he nevere so wel of lovyng preche,*
> *It made his hewe a-day ful ofte greene.*
> *So shop it that hym fil that day a teene*
> *In love, for which in wo to bedde he wente,*
> *And made, er it was day, ful many a wente.*
>
> *The swalowe Proigne, with a sorowful lay,*
> *Whan morwen com, gan make hire waymentynge,*
> *Whi she forshapen was; and ever lay*
> *Pandare abedde, half in a slomberynge,*
> *Til she so neigh hym made hire cheterynge*
> *How Tereus gan forth hire suster take,*
> *That with the noyse of hire he gan awake,*
>
> *And gan to calle, and dresse hym up to ryse,*
> *Remembryng hym his erand was to doone*
> *From Troilus . . .*
>
> (57–73)

In Chaucer's Troy, the 'teene' of love seems contained and rapidly assimilated, as the Procne lines at the center of this little episode show us. Tragic 'waymentynge', appropriate to Ovidian passion and transformation, becomes the noise and 'cheterynge' (one of the Owl's favorite words for the Nightingale's sound) of the familiar morning, and Pandarus is ready to go about his business. In the lines bracketing those on the swallow, love-sickness changes from something which separates one from the world to an affliction that may cost you a day now and then: lie down for a while and you'll feel better.

Pandarus is not the only character to make grand passion seem a hearthside phenomenon. Particularly important in its effect upon the reader is Chaucer's presentation of Helen and, along with her, of Deiphebus and the other charming Trojans of the second and third books. Here, in a part of the work owing comparatively little to Boccaccio, we feel love to be a snugly human thing, securely colleted with, but also blurred into, friendship. The situation is this. Pandarus, after his early exercises in persuasion, prying, and negotiating, has decided it is time for the lovers to have an interview. His first move in arranging this is to ask Troilus which of his brothers he loves best, 'as in thi verray hertes privetee' (II, 1397). Now that, it seems to me, is a rather curious phrase, suggesting something like a fraternal variety of *derne love*. Rather curious: no more than that. Given the general similarity of the language of love and the language of friendship in Chaucer's literary culture, it seems unlikely that any fourteenth-century reader was puzzled or startled by the phrase; doubtless few twentieth-century readers pause here. The phrase slips by, but quietly does its work. The whole inquiry is a bit odd in the way that phrase is just a bit odd. There is no practical reason why it must be his friend's *favorite* brother Pandarus uses to further Troilus's love. This is merely a managerial flourish, but a flourish suggesting the values of Chaucer's Troy: love of a brother, of a friend, of a lady, are things like one another and appropriate contexts for one another. In any case, the answer to Pandarus's question is Deiphebus; and Deiphebus, it transpires, is not only Troilus's favorite among his brothers, but Pandarus's second best friend. What is more, Pandarus himself is the man whom, after his brother Troilus, Deiphebus most loves. Pandarus sets to work and presents his cover story. He explains to Deiphebus that the favor he is asking is for Criseyde, a lady in this town who is his niece. But in Troy, and especially in this episode which brings the lovers together, all one's friends turn out to be each other's friends as well. Troilus's favorite brother is splendidly emphatic in his reaction:

> 'O, is nat this,
> That thow spekest of to me thus straungely,
> Criseÿda, my frend?' He seyde, 'Yis'.
> 'Than nedeth', quod Deiphebus, 'hardyly,
> Namore to speke, for trusteth wel that I
> Wol be hire champioun with spore and yerde;
> I roughte nought though alle hire foos it herde . . .'
> (II, 1422–8)

The scheme for the meeting of the two lovers involves a piling up of solicitude. Troilus may hope Criseyde will show some pity for the suffering love causes him, and Troilus, because he is ill, arouses the compassion of the other kindly folk gathered in this house. Those other folk are, moreover, filled with sympathy for Criseyde in her difficulties with Poliphete. There are comic curlicues of compassion: Chaucer invites the reader to smile at the absurdity of anyone taking the trouble to urge Troilus to be a friend to Criseyde (II, 1553–4); Criseyde sees and, one assumes, savors the ridiculousness of other persons discussing cures for Troilus's malady when she, who would be his best physician, is in the room (II, 1581–2). The Trojans' kindliness is engagingly mixed up with small vanities and competitions (II, 1578–87). Thus we can feel slightly and comfortably superior to it and be just a bit patronizing: this is not a *caritas* of which we must stand in awe.

And here, in Deiphebus's house, we meet the extraordinary Helen of Chaucer's Troy. She is startling in one sense because of what she is not: the woman 'par cui li siegles est peior'.[9] Elsewhere in the *Troilus* we hear about the heroic queen: in the fifth book Diomede will emphasize both for us and for Criseyde the connection between the love of Paris and Helen and the great suffering there will be at Troy (V, 890–6); the narration also opens with the theme of destructive passion, Chaucer reminding us that the Greeks beseiged the city to avenge the taking of Helen (I, 61–3). But now, in the second book, at the time when Criseyde is coming to take a prince of Troy as her lover, we actually see Queen Helen, and here Helen is altogether domesticated. She is, like Deiphebus, a great friend, the loving 'suster' of her two loving brothers. (Helen is fond of the words 'brother' and 'sister'.)[10] She is as warmly sympathetic toward Criseyde in her supposed troubles with Poliphete as she is with Troilus in his *accesse*:

> Eleyne, which that by the hond hire held,
> Took first the tale, and seyde, 'Go we blyve';
> And goodly on Criseyde she biheld,
> And seyde, 'Joves lat hym nevere thryve,
> That doth yow harm, and brynge hym soone of lyve,
> And yeve me sorwe, but he shal it rewe,
> If that I may, and alle folk be trewe!'.
>
> (II, 1604–10)

Chaucer doesn't tell us this, but she seems to have put on a few pounds. It occurs to Deiphebus that Helen would be a handy person to number among Criseyde's friends, 'for she may leden Paris as hire leste' (II, 1449). Eros, the force behind those thousand ships and the siege, now drives a small, very convenient household appliance. Passion is something that facilitates kindness. How cosy this is – and, for the fearfulest wight that might be, how seductive. Could even the smallest mouse's heart be afraid of heroic love when *this* comfortable creature is Helen of Troy? Who would find Pandarus's jolly woe unendurable? And so love blurs into the ordinary and the comforting. As we move toward the consummation of the passion of hero and heroine, Chaucer's language makes the Criseyde who in Book III takes Troilus into her bed an echo, a fulfilment of the maternal Helen who tried to cheer the bed-ridden hero in the second book:

> *Eleyne, in al hire goodly softe wyse,*
> *Gan hym salue, and wommanly to pleye,*
> *And seyde, 'Iwys, ye moste alweies arise!*
> *Now, faire brother, beth al hool, I preye!'*
> *And gan hire arm right over his shulder leye,*
> *And hym with al hire wit to reconforte;*
> *As she best koude, she gan hym to disporte.*
> (II, 1667–73)

> *And therwithal hire arm over hym she leyde,*
> *And al foryaf, and ofte tyme hym keste.*
> *He thonked hire, and to hire spak, and seyde*
> *As fil to purpos for his hertes reste;*
> *And she to that answerde hym as hire leste,*
> *And with hire goodly wordes hym disporte*
> *She gan, and ofte his sorwes to comforte.*
> (III, 1128–34)

I must confess to a great fondness for Chaucer's Helen, and would be glad to linger over this portrayal. But there are several other things of considerable interest I want to discuss here as well. Three aspects of Chaucer's poem I have not touched on as yet work subtly to make life – and especially love – in Troy seem more cushioned and less demanding than Criseyde finally discovers them to be. These three are the use of meals, the use of space, and an odd trick of narrative structure. The last of these is the most complex and, I think, the one to consider first.

As hero and heroine progress toward their first night together, two rather like scenes are presented in close succession: these are, of course, the one in which Troilus, put to bed in his brother's house, is visited by Criseyde, and that in which Criseyde, put to bed in her uncle's house, is visited by Troilus. Chaucer's arrangement here lends itself to various sorts of explanations, but it seems to me particularly interesting when thought of as one of a group of doublings in this first half of the poem. One should consider especially: the way Troilus's second heroine-impressing ride past Criseyde's window follows pretty soon after his first; the two slowly, lovingly rendered embassies of Pandarus to his niece in Book II; the fact that here (as in Boccaccio) there are two accounts – the poet's and then Pandarus's – of how Troilus comes to tell his friend why he is suffering, and that the second, Pandarian account, being in part a fuller narrative, forces us to modify our understanding of what Pandarus knew when he entered Troilus's chamber. One might also pause here to consider one slightly odd thing about the way Chaucer's readers are made to experience Troilus's conversion to love. It is a single, sudden experience, that conversion, and in a moment it changes the hero's life forever. But because Troilus attempts to hide his feelings after seeing Criseyde in the temple, and Pandarus chooses to quote his friend's earlier statements,we hear some fifty lines of the jibes of Troilus, the mocker of love (I, 330–50, 908–28), after he has become Troilus, the woeful lover. Now cumulatively these doublings and overlappings I've cited are a bit confusing; we may not be perplexed while reading along, but we have a certain amount of trouble if we try to recall clearly just what happened when. Incidents meld with one another, and the experience of the reader attempting to keep things straight becomes somewhat like the heroine's experience in negotiating with her uncle. What with the strange suppleness of Pandarus's arguments, it is most difficult for Criseyde to be certain just where she stands in her dealings with him. (How well her sense of the Pandarian undertow is caught in that skittish exclamation: '"Nay, therof spak I nought, ha, ha!" quod she; / "As helpe me God, ye shenden every deel!"'' (II, 589–90).) She would have to listen with uncommon attentiveness to know precisely what she had assented to at any given moment in her conversations with the charming Pandarus; readers of Chaucer (fox that he is) would have to be extraordinarily vigilant if they expected to remember just where a given change occurred, a certain stage in the lovers' relationship was reached. The first half of *Troilus and Criseyde* is a narrative of attractive, warm, subtly contrasting and then blending greys. Things take a while to happen; we come to a corner, but suspect we've turned it before, or, thinking back, find it hard to recall just when a certain corner *was* turned, or say to ourselves, ah, here at last is a corner! only to find we're wrong. Changes tend to blur in the reader's mind, just as they surely ought to blur for someone like Criseyde, a timid widow who is to become a hero's lady.

The passage in which Criseyde does at last become the hero's lady – or, more exactly, the passage in which she confesses herself already yielded to him – is as lovely a comic exchange as Chaucer ever invented. At the deepest level, the reader's laughter here is celebratory laughter, but one ought to notice also how at this moment Chaucer plays with two things we have been discussing: the theme of the frightening heroic, and the blurring of important shifts. Troilus, as he enters his lady's bed for the first time, seems as absurdly unthreatening a figure as one could wish. He is of course not pretending to be weak here, had not planned to faint – but in the first half of the *Troilus* all things do conspire to bring the lovers together, and if one wanted to enter the bed of the fearfulest wight that might be, sorrow, fear, and a swoon would not be the worst of tactics: the lady is in command. Here, though, after the heroine receives the passive hero into her bed, hears his vows, grants him foregiveness, and before the sexual consummation, there is a reversal. For a moment, all Criseyde's persistent anxieties about the nature of love, about prince Troilus, about what I am calling the heroic, suddenly appear justified. Troilus takes Criseyde in his arms; she begins to quake like an aspen leaf; her newly revived lover, as insistent as that eagle was, is a sparrowhawk clutching its prey: '. . . Now be ye kaught, now is ther but we tweyne! / Now yeldeth yow, for other bote is non!' (III, 1207–8). But Criseyde's hovering fears are given this sudden justification only so that they may be climactically ridiculed and exorcized. And the speech destroying the threateningness of Troilus here is at once the speech in the poem we most like Criseyde for making, and the statement in the poem which forces us most directly to acknowledge that things *have* been blurry, that we don't know, or at least seem unable to recall, just when, just how, with just what understanding of the situation, a central decision *was* reached: 'Ne hadde I er now, my swete herte deere, / Ben yold, ywis, I were now nought heere!' (III, 1210–11).

Criseyde takes Troilus as her lover at her uncle's house, in the second of two nicely matched scenes. We are aware in both – in the scene at Deiphebus's house and in that at Pandarus's – of movement from larger to smaller rooms, and also of meals taken in common out there, in the great hall. Those meals, though they are not described in any detail, have their importance. One thing we know about grand, unhappy lovers is that they do not eat: in the first book, love has quite properly made Troilus's meat his foe (I, 485); in the fifth book, when

119

the hero is again out of joy, he will again cease to eat and drink (V, 1216). But Pandarus, one must never forget, is himself one of these lovers, and his modified hyperbole modifies our sense of the traditional phenomenon. Thus, these lines from the second of his visits to Criseyde's palace:

> *Therwith she lough, and seyde, 'Go we dyne'.*
> *And he gan at hymself to jape faste,*
> *And seyde, 'Nece, I have so gret a pyne*
> *For love, that everich other day I faste —'*
> *And gan his beste japes forth to caste,*
> *And made hire so to laughe at his folye,*
> *That she for laughter wende for to dye.*
>
> *And whan that she was comen into halle,*
> *'Now, em', quod she, 'we wol go dyne anon.'* . . .
>
> (II, 1163–71)

Notice not only the deheroicizing jest, but its context: laughter, and 'go we dyne . . . we wol go dyne anon'. Communal meals mark the arrangements by which the Trojan lovers are brought together: Criseyde's dinner, the dinner at Deiphebus's house, and, finally Pandarus's supper. Love itself, happy, consummated love, is a feast (III, 1228, 1312) and of course *feast* unobtrusively suggests both the religion of love and love as joyful friendliness. In the poem's rising action, Criseyde finds love to be not a *minnegrotte* in the wilderness where two noble hearts can be all in all to one another, and no food is, no food need be taken, but a small room near that hall where loving friends have dined together.

Architecturally, those small rooms, the little closet Criseyde occupies on the night of her visit to Pandarus, and the chamber where Troilus lies at his brother's house, would almost certainly have been located off to one side of the hall in which host and guests ate their meal.[11] But linguistically, each of them is the small area *within*: one moves *in* to and then *out* from the little chamber into the hall again. Criseydan love is contained, secure, unfrightening: the curtained bed in the little room in the walled city whose name rhymes endlessly with joy.[12]

The city, the friend's house, the chamber, the bed, sexual union The movement of the first half of *Troilus and Criseyde* is centripetal, that of the second centrifugal: Criseyde goes to the Greek camp, Troilus to the eighth sphere. (How fine that the hero looks back to 'this litel spot of erthe, that with the se / *Embraced* is' (V, 1815–16).) In the second part of the work those gestures which earlier seemed over-large are appropriate, and Troilus becomes the most dignified of the major characters. Now Criseyde tries to be more than she is. In Book IV she really does think, for a moment, that she would have used that sword to kill herself; she speaks the truth Gottfried's noble hearts know: 'hym byhoveth somtyme han a peyne, / That serveth Love, if that he wol have joye' (IV, 1305–6); for the first time, she names the god of Love (IV, 1216).

Now Criseyde takes a high tragic heroine's attitude toward the trivially comforting. She is visited, as in Boccaccio, by a group of Trojan women who have learned of the proposed exchange of prisoners. In Chaucer's poem, this social gathering, coming early in the falling action, recalls the dinner at Deiphebus's house not too long before the lovers' period of joy. Again there is the group of well-meaning, slightly self-important guests. One is glad that Criseyde will see her father again; another is sorry, 'For al to litel hath she with us be' (IV, 690); a third hopes Criseyde will bring peace – may God guide her when she goes (691–3). Chaucer's Helen might have enjoyed a visit from such women, but now Criseyde, the widow whom we first saw troubled and friendless, and who will later be vulnerably placed 'with wommen fewe, among the Grekis stronge' (V, 688), now Criseyde certainly does not like their company. At least as important as the heroine's desire to be free of her visitors is the narrator's scorn for these harmless comforters. They are 'fooles', these ladies (IV, 715). In fact, they are not called ladies at all; apparently 'wommen' is quite good enough for them, even if the word has to be used three times in one stanza (IV, 680–6).

It is both funny and moving, this new contempt for those who 'usen frendes to visite' (IV, 681). Grief at what is happening rechannels itself as satire. One wants to strike out at something, and these Trojan women are, alas, the available targets. But the women are more than this; they represent what has already been lost: the pleasures of the ordinary. A liking for that kind of thing ought to be behind us now, and since we readers find ourselves more sympathetic to those trivial comforters than is either Criseyde or the narrator, the change strikes us with especial force. *We* are the ones hopping along behind, not having yet made the adjustment, not quite willing to dismiss diverse folk speaking diversely as rash, intruding fools.

Criseyde is ahead of us here. But she will not be able to bear heroic isolation for very long. In the last book she'll try to lessen her guilt, both in Troilus's eyes and her own, by treating friendliness as a fall-back position: certainly she will never hate Troilus, 'And frendes love, that shal ye han of me, / And my good work, al sholde I lyven evere . . .' (V, 1080–1); she asks him for his good word and his friendship always, 'For trewely, while that my life may dure, / As for a frend ye may in me assure . . .' (V, 1623–4). 'Frendes love': we will recall Pandarus's assurance that Troilus desired nothing but Criseyde's 'frendly cheere' (II, 332) and the granting of her 'love of frendshipe' (II, 962) as Criseyde began to move toward taking Troilus as a lover. In other words, she is now, perhaps without much conviction, trying to descend from love in the easy, ambiguously marked stages by which she ascended to it. This can't be done; the way up may seem a meandering path, but the way down is a cliff.

None of this excuses Criseyde: she forsakes Troilus who ought not to be forsaken. She is charming, and her mind is quick where his is slow and weighty; but finally it matters that Criseyde's is a smaller soul than Troilus's. He can bear pressures which she cannot; he thinks more important thoughts than she does. And again, it is Troilus whose experience in the work as a whole represents our experience in the world. What, then, is the reason for what I have been discussing in these pages, that deep Criseydan counter-current in the poem? Well, any question about the reason for a pattern in a complex narrative can be answered in a good number of ways: such a question is as bad as it is inevitable. Here one sort of answer is, I think, obvious enough: something which allows us to experience a complex situation in more than one way but does not cloud the central moral truth of that situation enriches the work of which it is a part. But having said this, I must confess another kind of answer – more speculative, if less pompous – appeals to me strongly.

If one should ask, for what sort of character Geoffrey Chaucer appears to have the greatest affinity, the reply would likely be (certainly mine would be), the Theseus sort of character. J. A. Burrow's discussion of Ricardian poetry is very useful here. Chaucer, Burrow suggests, can be thought of as, like his greatest contemporaries, .a poet of middle age, his attitudes essentially those of the *Knight's Tale*:

> The Knight (like his Theseus . . .) is of an age when he no longer shares the preoccupations of Palamon or Arcite (or the

Squire) and does not yet share the preoccupations of the aged Egeus. From his middle position among the three ages of man, the Knight can appreciate both the passionate Venerian vision of the young men and also the old man's Saturnine vision of earth as nothing but a 'thurghfare ful of wo'. But neither of these intensely serious visions is the poem's vision . . .

[Such Chaucerian figures as Theseus, Pandarus and Harry Baily] with their characteristic 'jovial' wisdom, embody an image of man which is not heroic, not romantic, and not at all 'monkish'. It is an image of 'high eld' which stands at the centre of Ricardian poetry, an ideal of 'measure' which involves that sober acceptance of things as they are which Theseus advocates . . .[13]

What does all of this have to do with Criseyde? Well, here some schematizing may prove helpful. If I present the sequence Palamon (and with Palamon, Troilus and Arcite) – Theseus – Egeus in the form A – B – A, the stages of heroic intensity on either side of the Thesean interheroic stage, then Criseyde might be placed at the very beginning of the sequence as the figure of a preheroic or subheroic life. My group would then be: Criseyde – Palamon (Troilus) – Theseus – Egeus, and this I might present in the form B – A – B – A – or more clearly:

Criseyde

Palamon (Troilus)

Theseus

Egeus.

Theseus and Criseyde are at different latitudes, let us say, but the same longitude: there are odd, almost comic, likenesses. 'The sober acceptance of things as they are': with the adjective deleted, Burrow's good, sounding formulation will serve for Criseyde. Consider for a moment two passages about not *grucching*. Why, Theseus asks, should we *grucchen* because good Arcite has left the foul prison of this life? Why do Palamon and Emily *grucchen* 'of his welfare'? It is wisdom, rather, 'to maken vertu of necessitee, / And take it weel that we may nat eschue' (*CT*. I, 3058–63, 3041–2). Pandarus asks Criseyde to stay at his house. It is raining fiercely. Criseyde's mind does not turn to the arrangements of Jupiter, prince and cause of all things; she thinks simply:

123

> *'As good chep may I dwellen here,*
> *And graunte it gladly with a frendes chere,*
> *And have a thonk, as grucche and than abide;*
> *For hom to gon, it may nought wel bitide'.*
>
> (III, 641–4)

'As good chep'. There is acceptance in both passages, but not the same
sobriety: sobriety is a function of latitude. Like Theseus, Criseyde
quotes that proverb about making a virtue of necessity (IV, 1586),
and we can listen for the Theseanism – debased, parody Theseanism,
if you will – of

> *'. . . But syn I se ther is no bettre way,*
> *And that to late is now for me to rewe,*
> *To Diomede algate I wol be trewe'*
>
> (V, 1069–71)

Would it not be Thesean wisdom for Emily to have thoughts *something*
like these?

Though I can't quite convince myself that Chaucer would have liked
my character-chart, I do find it helpful to consider our poem's complex
attitude toward its heroine in connexion with that odd similarity of
the Thesean and the Criseydan. In themselves more limited goods,
the sources of comfort in the earlier phase are like things nobly
championed in the later one. Friendliness is related to sober pity;
snug sociability as a reassuring setting resembles public ceremony as
a validating setting. We consider the lovers again, and say, yes, it is
better to be Troilus than Criseyde: he is the higher, the more fully
human of the two. And yet the lower of these two is in certain ways
the one closer to a type higher, more fully human than either – and a
type one guesses to be, of all types, the one most congenial to
Chaucer. If all of this sounds rather like a Romantic sequence of
innocence – experience – higher innocence . . . well, one might
brazen it out and say, simply, why shouldn't it? But I wonder
whether this shadowy dialectic isn't more complex still. Theseus is in
an obvious sense greater than Troilus, we have said – more richly
human, more intelligent, more Chaucerian. Yet one may feel that
Troilus's single-minded intensity is a more profound sort of response
to the world than the humane irony of Theseus – or of his creator.
Perhaps the man who sees both sides and makes the best of things
always suspects, 'as in his verray hertes privetee' (II, 1397), that he's
less in earnest than the fanatic. It is ultimately the hyperbolists and
radicals who turn out to be right. Criseyde is oddly like Theseus;

Troilus less oddly like Egeus or the Parson. Chaucer is a poet of the unheroic, but a poet of the unheroic who knows (or suspects) the heroes are finally correct. Chaucer's two greatest works conclude with reversals. He is the poet of what is not the highest thing and must at the very end be given up. Much of the strength of the Criseydan strain in the *Troilus* comes from the peculiar affinity of Criseyde and what finally is not just Thesean man, but Chaucerian man. She and not the poem's hero may be the more profoundly autobiographical creation.

Notes

The text of the *Troilus*

Barry Windeatt

1   R. K. Root, *The Book of Troilus and Criseyde* (Princeton, 1926), pp. lxx–lxxxi; cf. also his *The Textual Tradition of Chaucer's Troilus*, Chaucer Society, First Series XCIX (London, 1916), hereafter abbreviated to *TT*.

2   F. N. Robinson, *The Complete Works of Geoffrey Chaucer*, 2nd edition (London, 1957).

3   A. Brusendorff, *The Chaucer Tradition* (London, 1925), p. 171. For articles on the literary merits of what are seen as authorial differences between the MSS, cf. also C. A. Owen, 'The Significance of Chaucer's Revisions of *Troilus and Criseyde*', *MP*, LV (1957–8), 1–5; and 'Minor Changes in Chaucer's *Troilus and Criseyde*', (in) *Chaucer and Middle English Studies in Honor of R. H. Robbins*, edited by B. Rowland (London, 1974), pp. 303–19. Cf. further Daniel Cook, 'The Revision of Chaucer's *Troilus*: The Beta Text', *Chaucer Review*, 9 (1974–5), 51–62.

4   For a lucid survey of recent trends, cf. Anne Hudson's chapter 'Middle English', (in) *Editing Medieval Texts*, edited by A. G. Rigg (New York and London, 1977), pp. 34–57.

5   Some other way of referring to the MSS groups is needed to replace Root's method of Greek letters, because they or any other sequence of letters imply a progression, as Mr Ramsay knew when he struggled to get from Q to R in *To The Lighthouse*. The three main groups will hereafter be denominated neutrally Ph*etc*, Cp*etc*, and R*etc*, after one MS which is the constant supporter of each grouping through the poem and from which variants will be cited. The terms 'α', 'γ', 'β' will be used only in reference to Root's theories. The sigils follow Root's usage except A becomes Ad, D becomes Du.

6   Cf. 'dolcemente a cantare in cotal guisa' (3.73). All reference to *Filostrato* (*Fil*) is to *Tutte le opere di Giovanni Boccaccio*, edited by V. Branca, vol. II (Milan, 1964).

7   *Chaucerian and other Pieces*, edited by W. W. Skeat (Oxford, 1897), p. 123.
8   e.g. one-word variations over related diction (*wo* / *sorwe; woful* / *sorwful* (IV, 794; 843; 1134); *ioye* / *blisse* (IV, 835; 1250; 1323); *tel* / *seye* (IV, 173; 484)); or syntactical variations in Ph*etc*: e.g. for IV, 322 ('Forthi no fors is though the, body sterve') Ph*etc* read 'Forthy no fors whan þat þe body sterve'; for IV, 102 ('I may hire haue right soone douteles') Ph*etc* read 'I may her have for þat is douteles'.
9   Many R*etc* readings are easier, probably scribal: e.g. for III, 529 ('In this matere bothe *fremed* and tame') R*etc* reads '*wilde* and tame'; or for III, 1115 ('they gan to frote and *wete* his temples tweyne'), where *Fil* has 'la faccia bagnandogli' (4.19), R*etc* reads instead 'and *ek* his temples' which seems easier and inferior in context.
10 Thus in IV, 570, which is one of Root's principal cases of three-fold revision:
    (Ph*etc*) I haue her honour lever ʒet þan me   (Ph ʒet lever)
    (Cp*etc*) I moste hire honour leuere han than me
    (R*etc*) l must hyr honor leuer saue than me   (R *kepe* for *saue*)
The Cp*etc* reading, differing only in *saue*/*han*, is an easier reading for R*etc* (note that *saue* provokes variation by R itself). Ph*etc* is probably a more corrupted scribal version. The inferior, easier variations can be explained as a scribal progression *away* from one authentic version rather than an authentic, successive progression *through* three indifferent versions.
11 R*etc* reads (in J):
    But natheles a trewe was ther take
    At Grekys requeste and tho they gonnen trete (gret J)
    Of prisoners a chaunge forto make . . .
Cp*etc* reads:
    Of Priamus was ʒeue at Grekes requeste (a greke Cp)
    A tyme of trewe and tho they gonnen trete
    Hire prisoners to chaungen meste and leste . . .
The latter is perhaps an earlier attempt to translate 'Chiese Priamo triegua e fugli data / e cominciossi . . . / di permutar prigioni'. H₃ reads 'To Pryamus whas yeven at his Requeste', possibly even earlier translation, although perhaps accidental in this inventive scribe.
12 After IV, 28, Cp, Cl, Du H₁ have a rubric: 'Explicit liber Tercius. Incipit Liber Quartus'.
13 This stanza is found between II, 1750 and 1751 (R, f. 39ʳ). It is metrically deficient in the first line, somewhat inappropriate to its context, and is preceded by a repetition of ll. 1576–7 (cf. Root's discussion, *TT*, pp. 25–6).
14 More than one authorial archetype possibly existed, at a time when copies were rapidly proliferating, and the extant MSS themselves show scribes furthering 'horizontal' influence between texts: S1 contains a text intelligently edited between the Cp*etc* and R*etc* traditions, and the

fluctuating identity of Ph*etc* suggests how scribes switched and patched, using exemplars from different traditions. From their corrections scribes knew some MSS offered better readings in certain lines, which are left blank to be filled in or corrected over erasure.

15   Cf. *The English Works of John Gower*, edited by G. C. Macaulay, E.E.T.S., E.S. 81–2 (1900–1), pp. cxxvii–clxvii ('Text and Manuscripts').

16   Cf. G. H. Russell, 'Some Aspects of the Process of Revision in *Piers Plowman*', (in) *Piers Plowman: Critical Approaches*, edited by S. S. Hussey (London, 1969), pp. 27–49.

17   Machaut rarely wrote out his own works, cf. S. Williams, 'An Author's Role in Fourteenth Century Book Production', *Romania* XC (1969), 433–54. But holographs of Petrarch and Boccaccio indicate they revised earlier copies of their work, cf. G. Pasquali, *Storia della Tradizione e Critica del Testo* (Florence, 2nd edition, 1952), pp. 438ff. Boccaccio made changes in a copy of the *Decameron* which he transcribed some 17 years after the work was first completed, cf. V. Branca and P. G. Ricci, *Un Autografo del Decameron (Codice Hamiltoniano 90)* (Padova, 1962).

18   Deguilleville saw the first, stolen draft of his work circulated against his will, and to correct it he was obliged to issue a new one, cf. *Pilgrimage of the Life of Man*, edited by F. J. Furnivall, E.E.T.S., E.S., LXXVII (1899), ll. 237ff. and 267ff.

The lesson of the *Troilus*: Chastisement and Correction

Alan T. Gaylord

1   *Experience and Its Mode* (Cambridge, 1933), p. 33.

2   All quotations from Chaucer's works are from *The Works of Geoffrey Chaucer*, edited by F. N. Robinson (Boston, revised edition, 1957).

3   *Romaunt*, l. 3331; *Roman*, l. 3095. The two texts may most conveniently be studied in *The Romaunt of the Rose and the Roman de la Rose. A Parallel-Text Edition*, edited by Ronald Sutherland (Oxford, 1967).

4   'Friendship in Chaucer's *Troilus*', *Chaucer Review*, 3 (1969), 239–64.

5   'The Ending of *Troilus*', in *Speaking of Chaucer* (London, 1970), p. 92. Cf. Donaldson's 'Chaucer and the Elusion of Clarity,' in *Essays and Studies 1972*, N.S. 25 (London, 1972), 42: 'For Chaucer truth was never simple, always so qualified that the only way to express it satisfactorily was to mix statements of fact with many contradictory truths.'

6   'The Hero of the *Troilus*,' *Speculum*, 37 (1962), 578.

7   Wolfram von Eschenbach, *Parzival*, I, 4; translated by Helen M. Mustard and Charles E. Passage (New York, 1961), p. 5.

8   George Lyman Kittredge, *Chaucer and His Poetry* (Cambridge, Massa-

chusetts, 1915), pp. 112–21; Donaldson, *Chaucer's Poetry: An Anthology for the Modern Reader* (New York, 1958), pp. 975, 976.

9   Cf. G. T. Shepherd: 'The *argumentum* of the poem depends upon a melancholy, unsensationalised view of life, compounded out of a Christian quietism and a faintly sentimental stoicism'; *'Troilus and Criseyde'*, in *Chaucer and Chaucerians. Critical Studies in Middle English Literature.* edited by D. S. Brewer (London, 1966), p. 73.

10   *The Allegory of Love* (London, 1936), p. 43.

11   *'Troilus and Criseyde: a Reconsideration,'* in *Patterns of Love and Courtesy. Essays in Memory of C. S. Lewis,* edited by John Lawlor (London, 1966), p. 88.

12   *The Strumpet Muse. Art and Morals in Chaucer's Poetry* (London, 1976), pp. 29–30. He cites Salter approvingly, along with another ally, Joseph E. Gallagher, who had described the *Troilus* as 'at least in part, a complex reflection of its author's attempts to evade the strict terms of medieval religion'; 'Theology and Intention in Chaucer's *Troilus,*' *Chaucer Review*, 7 (Summer 1972), 66.

13   *Chaucer: The Knight's Tale and the Clerk's Tale* (London, 1962), p. 70.

14   'Chaucer's Tender Trap: the *Troilus* and the "Yonge, Fresshe Folkes",' *EM*, 15 (Rome, 1964), 25–45.

15   Root, *The Textual Tradition*, The Chaucer Society, 1st series, 99 (London, 1916), 217 – the relationship of texts with respect to this addition is discussed, pp. 216–21; Root, *The Book of Troilus and Criseyde* (Princeton, 1926), pp. 517–20; Patch, 'Troilus on Predestination,' *JEGP*, 17 (1918), 414–20; Curry, 'Destiny in *Troilus and Criseyde*', repr, in *Chaucer Criticism II. Troilus and Criseyde & The Minor Poems*, edited by Richard J. Schoeck and Jerome Taylor (Notre Dame, Indiana, 1961), pp. 55–7 – Patch's essay is in danger of slipping from sight (his more general piece on 'Troilus on Determinism' has been salvaged for the Schoeck and Taylor anthology, pp. 71–85), but is not dated, is learned and judicious, and is clearly and engagingly written; Gordon, *The Double Sorrow* (Oxford, 1970), pp. 42–6.

16   Cf. John S. P. Tatlock, 'The Epilog of Chaucer's *Troilus,*' *MP*, 18 (April 1921), 119–23, who discusses other medieval works which call for correction.

17   *John Gower. Moral Philosopher and Friend of Chaucer* (New York, 1964); esp. ch. 5, 'Gower and Chaucer,' pp. 204–302.

18   Martin M. Crow and Clair C. Olson, editors, *Chaucer Life-Records* (Oxford, 1966), pp. 54, 60, 282, and 284. A mainpernor was one who gave 'surety for a prisoner's appearance in court on a specified day' (*OED*).

19   Listed by George Sarton, *Introduction to the History of Science*, 3, pt. 2 (Washington, 1948), 1413.

20   VIII, 2941–57*; edited by G. C. Macaulay, *The English Works of John Gower*, 2 (Early English Text Society, 1901), 466.

21   There is some conjecture that there may have been two Ralph Strodes,

but A. B. Emden thinks that the 'biographical particulars do not seem to warrant this dichotomy'; *A Biographical Register of the University of Oxford to A.D. 1500*, 3 (Oxford, 1959), 1808.

22   *Responsiones ad argumenta Radulfi Strode* and *Responsio ad decem questiones magistri Richardi Strode*, in *Johannis Wyclif. Opera Minora*, edited by Johann Loserth (London, 1913), pp. 175–200, 398–404.

23   'His *Consequentiae* and *Obligationes* were used as prescribed texts in the University of Padua during the second half of 15th century,' Emden, *A Biographical Register*, 3, 1807.

24   Ed. Loserth, p. 181. Wyclif goes on to allow 'conditional necessity,' however.

25   *John Wyclif. A Study of the English Medieval Church*, 2 (Oxford, 1926), 129.

26   Book III, chapter iv; edited by Walter W. Skeat, *Chaucerian and Other Pieces* (Oxford, 1897), p. 123.

27   Cf. J. A. W. Bennett, 'Gower's "Honeste Love",' in *Patterns of Love and Courtesy*, edited by Lawlor, pp. 107–21.

28   'Zeles' as 'fervent love' is supported by the *OED*, which cites the 1382 Wyclif Bible; note also the c.1400 *Rule of St Benet*, also cited: 'as there is an euyll zele, loue, or affeccyon the whiche departyth one from god . . . so there is a zele or affeccion . . . the which departyth one from synne.'

Realism in *Troilus and Criseyde* and the *Roman de la Rose*

James I. Wimsatt

1   'Medieval and Modern in Chaucer's Troilus and Criseyde', *PMLA*, 92 (1977), 203–16.

2   The point is implicit, for instance, in T. S. Eliot's 'Tradition and the Individual Talent', in which he speaks of the essential role of tradition in literary creation. Similarly, Northrop Frye, *Anatomy of Criticism* (Princeton, N. J.: Princeton Univ. Press, 1957), p. 97, declares, 'Poetry can only be made out of other poems; novels out of other novels'.

3   E. D. Hirsch, Jr., *Validity in Interpretation* (New Haven: Yale Univ. Press, 1967), p. 104.

4   See Hirsch, pp. 78–89, 102–11.

5   For a useful, though dated, survey of the medieval French tradition of Ovid, see Gaston Paris, 'Chrétien Legouais et autres traducteurs ou imitateurs d'Ovide', *Histoire littéraire de la France*, 29 (1885; rpt. Paris: Librairie Universitaire, 1900), 455–525. See also Ernest Langlois, *Origines et sources du Roman de la Rose* (1890; rpt. Geneva: Slatkine Rpts., 1973), pp. 21–25; and Robert Bossuat, *Drouart la Vache: Traducteur d'André le Chapelain* (Paris: Champion, 1926), *passim*.

6   Citations of the *Roman de la Rose* herein refer to the edition of Ernest Langlois, Société des anciens textes français, 5 vols. (Paris: Champion, 1914–24).

7   Quoted from *Ovid: The Art of Love and Other Poems*, translated by J. H. Mozley, Loeb Classical Library (Cambridge, Mass.: Harvard Univ. Press, 1962), p. 201.

8   See Langlois, *Origines*, pp. 71–4.

9   *Origines*, pp. 119–25, 153.

10   *Origines*, pp. 27–8.

11   *Origines*, pp. 28–31. The basis in *Pamphilus* that Langlois claims for the character of Ami is not impressive. As he grants, p. 30, the inspiration for Ami may come more directly from another member of the Art of Love family, Andreas's *De amore*.

12   'The *Pamphilus* Tradition in Ruiz and Chaucer', *Philological Quarterly*, 46 (1967), 457–70. Garbáty translates *Pamphilus* in *Chaucer Review*, 2 (1967), 108–34. The work is edited, among other places, in Gustave Cohen, *La 'Comédie' latine en France au xii᷉ siècle*, 2 vols. (Paris, 1931), II, 166–223 (with trans. into French).

13   *Amores* I, viii. See Paris, p. 488.

14   *Philological Quarterly*, 46, 460–1. The part that Pandarus plays in the consummation scene, like the scene itself, has no real counterpart in the *Filostrato*.

15   Editors find sources in Ovid for the following speeches of Pandarus: *Troilus* II, 393–405 in *Ars amatoria* II, 113–18; II, 1023–6 in *Ars* I, 463–8; III, 1634 in *Ars* II, 11–13; I, 946–9 in *Remedia amoris* 45–6; and IV, 421–4 in *Remedia* 135–44, 149–50, 205–6, 214–40, and 452. And they see the following lines spoken by Pandarus as originating in the *Roman de la Rose*: *Troilus* I, 960–1 in *Roman* 2245–6 (God of Love); I, 969 in 12760 (La Vieille); III, 292–4 in 7055–7 (Raison) and 12179–83 (Abstinence); III, 329 in 8003–4 (Ami) and III, 1634 in 8261–4 (Ami). Citations of Chaucer's works herein are to F. N. Robinson, ed., *The Works of Geoffrey Chaucer*, 2nd edition (Boston: Houghton, 1957).

16   This group of works is most fully treated in Winthrop Wetherbee, *Platonism and Poetry in the Twelfth Century* (Princeton, N. J.: Princeton Univ. Press, 1972). Valuable recent studies of central figures in them are George D. Economou, *The Goddess Natura in Medieval Literature* (Cambridge, Mass.: Harvard Univ. Press, 1972), and Jane Chance Nitzsche, *The Genius Figure in Antiquity and the Middle Ages* (New York: Columbia Univ. Press, 1975).

17   See Langlois, *Origines*, pp. 148–50.

18   Numerous critics have asserted the unity of the *Roman*, but not explicitly on the basis I suggest here; that is, of literary frame-of-reference or genre. The poems of Guillaume and Jean are continuous and largely harmonious, and they are of the same kind.

19   *Bernardi Silvestris de mundi universitate libri duo*, edited by Carl S. Barach

and Johann Wrobel (Innsbruck, 1876), I, iii. 315–36; II, ix. 11–28; trans. Winthrop Wetherbee, *The Cosmographia of Bernardus Silvestris* (New York: Columbia Univ. Press, 1973), pp. 82–3, 110–11.

20   In this garden, says Bernard, I, iii. 333–4, man had his first home. Like Eden according to tradition, Granusion is located in the east, as Bernard states twice: I, iii. 315; II, ix. 14–15.

21   *Alain de Lille: Anticlaudianus*, edited by Robert Bossuat (Paris: Vrin, 1955), I, 54–106; trans. William H. Cornog, *The Anticlaudian of Alain de Lille* (Phila.: Univ. of Pennsylvania Diss., 1935), pp. 53–4.

22   Cornog, p. 55; Bossuat I, 124–5: 'In res umbracula rerum / Vertit'.

23   *De planctu naturae*, in *Patrologiae cursus completus: Series latina* (*PL*), edited by J. P. Migne, vol. 210 (Paris, 1855), col. 453. I quote from the translation of Douglas Moffat, *The Complaint of Nature* (1908; rpt. Archon, 1972), p. 44.

24   Moffat, p. 45; *PL* 210, col. 454.

25   Moffat, pp. 46–8; *PL* 210, col. 455.

26   Carnal love which does not have procreation as its purpose, whether or not it results in offspring, I take it, is of its nature sterile. The father of Jocus is identified in MSS alternatively as Antigamus or Antigenius (see Nitzsche, p. 164, n. 26). Either name indicates carnal love perverted from procreative ends.

27   *PL* 210, cols. 459–60; Moffat, pp. 56–8.

28   For the garden description in *PF* 183–294, Chaucer utilizes both a description in Boccaccio's *Teseida* that is largely based on the *Roman de la Rose*, and the *Roman* directly. See notes of Robinson, p. 794, and D. S. Brewer, *Geoffrey Chaucer: The Parlement of Foulys* (London: Nelson, 1960), pp. 106–8.

29   By virtue of the reference, ll. 6–10, Scipio's dream appears as the prototype for the dream in the *Roman*, just as it obviously is for the dream in *PF* in the light of the prefatory summary of Scipio's vision, ll. 29–84.

30   The opening of the *Échecs* includes an allegorical journey, and an appearance of Nature, who is described at length in accordance with Alan's depiction. The *Échecs* has not had a complete edition. I follow the summary of Stanley L. Galpin, '*Les Eschez Amoureux*: A Complete Synopsis with Unpublished Extracts', *Romantic Review*, 11 (1920), 283–307, and the expanded translation of the poem (its first 4873 ll.) by John Lydgate, *Reson and Sensuallyte*, edited by Ernest Sieper, 2 vols, Early English Text Society, Extra Series, nos. 84 and 89 (London: Oxford Univ. Press, 1901–3).

31   In the *Échecs* the two sons of Venus are identified as Cupid and Deduit. The poet, then, sees Deduit as a French equivalent of Alan's Jocus. The fact that translators identify both personifications, Jocus and Deduit, as 'Mirth' supports, at some remove but interestingly, the identification the *Échecs* poet makes of Guillaume's Deduit with Alan's Jocus. The Chaucerian *Romaunt of the Rose* renders Deduit as 'Mirth' consistently.

Moffat, p. 56, translates Jocus as 'Mirth', as does C. E. Bennett, trans., *Horace: The Odes and Epodes*, Loeb Classical Library (Cambridge, Mass.: Harvard Univ. Press, 1964), Ode I, 2, 34 (which is the *locus classicus* for the two sons of Venus).

32   The Garden of Deduit may also be connected with the gardens of the Chartrian allegories by way of their common relationship to biblical Eden. Bernard's Granusion explicitly and Alan's Garden of Nature by virtue of its characterization and its filiation with Granusion are identified with the 'paradisus voluptatis' – 'garden of pleasure' – of Genesis ii. 8, 15. Likewise there is much about Guillaume's garden that associates it with the scriptural paradise. John Fleming, *The Roman de la Rose* (Princeton, N. J.: Princeton Univ. Press, 1969), p. 60, calls it a 'post-lapsarian terrestrial paradise'; he notes the statement of A. Bartlett Giamatti, *The Earthly Paradise and the Renaissance Epic* (Princeton, N. J.: Princeton Univ. Press, 1966), p. 66, 'The image of the earthly paradise haunts the *Roman de la Rose*'. We may add that 'Jardin de Deduit' and 'Paradisus Voluptatis' have a neat ironic equivalence.

33   The God of Love's robe is covered with birds and beasts of many kinds, and all the blooming flowers of summer (878–94). Cf. the description in *De planctu*, *PL* 210, cols. 435–9; Moffat, pp. 11–18.

34   *Roman*, ll. 2971–95. Among the features of Raison which recall Lady Philosophy as she is described in Book I of the *Consolation* are her appearance from above, her burning eyes, her uncertain age and equivocal height, her impressive dignity, and her heavenly origin. The names Raison and Philosophia, of course, have a common relationship to 'Wisdom'.

35   Lady Philosophy represents both natural and superior wisdom. Accordingly, Prudence and Reason in *Anticlaudianus* (I, 270–325, 436–64), and Nature in *De planctu* (*PL* 210, 432–3), have traits directly derived from Boethius's description of Lady Philosophy.

36   Barach and Wrobel, II, v. 180–3; Wetherbee, *Cosmographia*, p. 103. The attribution of the torch to Venus is rare before Bernard. In earlier literature I have found but one example of Venus with torch (*fax*), *Amores* I, i. 7–8. Both bow and torch are generally attributed to Cupid in classical art and literature. In the *Roman* and Chaucer, on the other hand, the torch is seen consistently as belonging to Venus.

37   See René Wellek's discussion of 'type' as a concept in theories of realism, *Concepts of Criticism*, edited by Stephen G. Nichols, Jr. (New Haven: Yale Univ. Press, 1963), pp. 238–9, 242–6.

38   'Tradition and the Individual Talent', in *The Sacred Wood* (New York: Knopf, 1921), p. 43.

Paganism and pagan love in *Troilus and Criseyde*
John Frankis

1   Dante, *Inferno* i. 124–6; Virgil is speaking: 'for that Emperor who reigns above, because I was a rebel against his law, does not wish that there should be any entry into his city for me'. On medieval ideas about Virgil see Domenico Comparetti, *Vergil in the Middle Ages* (London, 1908, repr. 1966), especially pp. 96–103. All quotations from Chaucer in this paper are from *The Works of Geoffrey Chaucer*, edited by F. N. Robinson (2nd edition, London, 1957). I am inevitably indebted to the writings of many critics, but I have not attempted to trace every debt in this paper to its source and to give proper acknowledgement for every idea that I have developed.

2   See, for example, Dante, *Inferno* iv and *Paradiso* xix; for a recent survey of medieval theories on the fate of righteous pagans in relation to English literature see *St Erkenwald*, edited by R. Morse (Cambridge, 1975), Introduction pp. 19–31. Both Dante and *St Erkenwald* leave open the possibility of some kind of selective salvation for the righteous pagan.

3   See G. L. Kittredge, 'Chaucer's Discussion of Marriage', *MP* 9 (1912), 435–67, and D. W. Robertson Jr., *A Preface to Chaucer* (Princeton, 1962), pp. 275–6 and 470–2.

4   The story as narrated in Boccaccio's *Il Filocolo* is conveniently accessible in W. F. Bryan and G. Dempster, *Sources and Analogues of Chaucer's Canterbury Tales* (Chicago, 1941), pp. 377–83. In the version of the story in Boccaccio's *Decamerone* X.5 (presumably unknown to Chaucer) the husband is also motivated by a prudent fear of the powers of a man who can perform such magic: 'inducendomi ancora la paura del nigromante'. It is not certain that *Il Filocolo* was Chaucer's source for the Franklin's Tale, it is merely the closest known analogue; but the comparison with Boccaccio is illuminating even if this was not Chaucer's source.

5   *Mandeville's Travels*, edited by M. C. Seymour (Oxford, 1967), p. 192: 'But whan he saugh that he myghte not don it ne bryng it to an ende, he preyed to God of Nature that He wolde parforme that that he had begonne. And alle were it so that he was a payneme and not worthi to ben herd, yit God of His grace closed the mountaynes togydre.' See also G. Cary, *The Medieval Alexander* (Cambridge, 1956), p. 132 and note 52 (p. 296), who gives numerous references to the story, but perhaps underestimates its significance as an exemplum of God's preparedness to respond to pagan prayers addressed to the universal God of Nature.

Letters as a type of the formal level in *Troilus and Criseyde*

John McKinnell

1   *Nicholai Treveti Expositio Herculis Furentis*, edited by V. Ussani Jr. (Rome, 1959), pp. 4–5; the translation is mine. See also J. Norton-Smith, *Geoffrey Chaucer*, Medieval Authors Series (London, 1974), pp. 164–8, and for a modern expression of levels in terms of 'triangles', M. W. Bloomfield, 'Distance and Predestination in *Troilus and Criseyde*', P.M.L.A., 72 (1957), 14–26.

2   Throughout this article, citations from *Troilus and Criseyde* which have no source in Boccaccio's *Il Filostrato*, and therefore represent modifications of Chaucer's received material, will be indicated by an asterisk. All citations of Chaucer's works are from *The Works of Geoffrey Chaucer*, edited by F. N. Robinson, 2nd edition (Boston, 1957).

3   See *The House of Fiction*, edited by Leon Edel (London, 1957), especially pp. 101–2.

4   *Paston Letters and Papers of the Fifteenth Century*, edited by Norman Davis, Parts I–II (Oxford, 1971–6) (Part III not yet published), Introduction pp. xxxvii–xxxviii.

5   See K. Sisam, *Fourteenth Century Verse and Prose* (Oxford, 1921), pp. 160–1.

6   Ludolf von Hildesheim, *Summa dictaminum* I, printed in L. Rockinger, *Briefsteller und formelbücher*, 2 vols, *Quellen und Erörterungen zur Bayerischen und Deutschen Geschichte* (München, 1863, reprinted New York, 1961), I, 359 – the translation is mine. Rockinger includes one work by an Englishman ('Johannes Anglicus' – i.e. John of Garland) and one written by a foreigner at Canterbury (John of Bologna).

7   These and the following figures are approximate and include drafts, but not copies made 'for the record' at a later date.

8   Davis, no. 798, II, 442.

9   Davis, no. 415, I, 662–3.

10   Davis, I, 575.

11   Davis, no. 930, II, 615–8; cf. nos. 123, 230, 929 (I, 210–14, 382–9 and II, 613–15).

12   J. J. Murphy, 'A New Look at Chaucer and the Rhetoricians', *RES* New Series XV (1964), pp. 1–20, lists three *artes dictandi* written in England before Chaucer's death but not mentioned by Rockinger.

13   Rockinger I, pp. 9–28; translated in *Three Medieval Rhetorical Arts*, edited by J. J. Murphy (Univ. of California, 1971), pp. 5–25; for the rejection of Rockinger's attribution to Alberich, see C. H. Haskins, 'The Early *Artes dictandi* in Italy', in *Studies in Medieval Culture* (Oxford, 1929), pp. 170–92, especially 181–2.

14   Rockinger I, pp. 185–96.

15   See N. Denholm-Young, 'The Cursus in England', *Collected Pap*

(Cardiff, 1969), pp. 42–73; J. J. Murphy, 'Rhetoric in Fourteenth Century Oxford', *Medium Ævum* 34 (1965), pp. 1–20, and *Rhetoric in the Middle Ages* (Univ. of California, 1974), ch. V.

16 Exceptions to this plan may be seen in Hugh of Bologna, whose three-part scheme (*Exordium, Narracio, Conclusio*) is probably derived from pseudo-Alberich, and John of Garland, whose six-part scheme *(Exordium, Narratio, Partitio, Confirmatio, Confutatio, Conclusio)* comes from Cicero, *De Inventione* I, xiv (edited and translated by H. M. Hubbell, Loeb Classical Library (London and Harvard, 1949), pp. 40–41 and ff.).

17 *Il Filostrato*, II, stt. 96–106, 121–7, and VII, 52–75. All references to this poem are from *The Filostrato of Boccaccio*, edited and translated by N. E. Griffin and A. B. Myrick (Univ. of Pennsylvania, 1929).

18 *Il Fil.*, II, st. 96. Chaucer borrows the refusal to send a greeting at the beginning of Criseyde's last letter (V, 1592–6*), but does not make her name herself first.

19 *Il Fil.*, II, st. 107.

20 In particular, Boccaccio has a gap between Troilo's letter and her reply (suggesting indifference on her part?), which Chaucer removes; and his Narrator refers to her false excuses (*Il Fil.*, VII, st. 105, 1.3), while Chaucer makes it merely Troilus's opinion that her promises are empty (V, 1431*).

21 Robinson, p. 836, suggests that *Il Fil.*, VIII, stt. 5–6, indicates that she wrote again, but the reference here seems to be to Criseida's previous letter (*Il Fil.*, VII, 105).

22 See for example Geoffroi de Vinsauf, *Documentum de Arte Dictandi et Versificandi*, II, 1, 2–4, in E. Faral, *Les Arts Poétiques du XIIe et du XIIIe siècle* (Paris, 1924), pp. 268–9.

23 Compare *Il Fil.*, VII, st. 53, ll. 1–2; st. 69, ll. 1–5; st. 73, ll. 5–8.

24 E.g. her speech at III, 820–36,* with which compare *Boece*, II, prosa 4, 75–8 and 118–27.

25 J. J. Murphy, 'A New Look at Chaucer and the Rhetoricians', has argued that the *artes poeticae* were little known in England in Chaucer's day; but though this is undoubtedly true (except of Oxford) of most writers on the subject, Geoffroi de Vinsauf seems from the surviving MSS to have been more widely known. MSS of his works (the complete *Poetria Nova*, the *Documentum*, or both) from English sources of Chaucer's time or earlier include:

> Bodley Laud misc. 515, from Waltham Abbey, Essex.
> Bodley Digby 104, from Witham Charterhouse, Somerset.
> Balliol 263 fol., probably from Oxford.
> Trinity College Cambridge 609, from Holm Cultram Abbey, Cumbria.
> Trinity College Cambridge 624, from Dover Priory.
> Trinity College Cambridge 895, probably from the Dominican Friary in Leicester.

Corpus Christi College Cambridge 217, from Worcester Cathedral
Priory.

BM Harley 3775, from St Alban's Abbey.

Bodley misc. 2056, Glasgow Hunterian 511 and York Minster 42 are
English MSS of unknown provenance, and BM Harley 3582, BM
Harley 6504 and BM Add. 18,153 may also be English. The rendering of
Poetria Nova, 43–5 (see Faral p. 198, *Three Medieval Rhetorical Arts*, p. 34)
in *Troilus and Criseyde*, I, 1065–9* is too close to be dismissed as
coincidence – quite apart from Chaucer's famous reference to Geoffroi in
the *Nun's Priest's Tale* (*Canterbury Tales* B², 3347–52), which could, as
Murphy points out, demonstrate only a knowledge of Geoffroi's famous
lament on the death of Richard Coeur de Lion. I shall assume, therefore,
that Chaucer knew the works of Geoffroi de Vinsauf but none of the
other writers on *ars poetica*.

26 On *exclamatio*, see *Poetria Nova*, 1105–9 (Faral, p. 231, *Three Medieval
Rhetorical Arts*, p. 74 and note 76) and *Documentum*, II, 2, 25 (Faral, p.
276); on *interrogacio*, *Poetria Nova*, 1109–11; on *determinatio*, *Poetria Nova*,
1761–70 (Faral, p. 251, *Three Medieval Rhetorical Arts*, p. 96); on *conduplicatio*, *Poetria Nova*, 1169 (Faral, p. 233, *Three Medieval Rhetorical Arts*, p. 75
and note 76); the uses of *conduplicatio* described by *Documentum*, II, 2, 26
(Faral, p. 276) are particularly appropriate here: 'quando ex dolore,
quando ex amore, quando ex indignatione' – 'sometimes out of grief,
sometimes out of love, sometimes out of indignation'.

27 Geoffroi calls it *significatio per ambiguitatem*, see *Poetria Nova*, 1545–8
(Faral, p. 244, *Three Medieval Rhetorical Arts*, p. 87).

28 Criseyde's belated concern for her reputation (V, 1062–3*), and her
suggestion here that Troilus's love is less than genuine (V, 1614–7*)
may also be influenced by *Heroides*, XVII, 211–20 and 37–42.

29 Davis, no. 373, I, 603–4. Some other letters contain attitudes or
expressions similar to those in the poem's letters, e.g. Davis, nos. 351,
362, 415, 416, the opening of 418 and 781 (I, 571–3, 590–1, 662–3,
665–6, II, 425). An interesting contrast may be drawn with Richard
Calle's letter to his wife, Margery Paston (Davis, no. 861, II, 498–500),
in which the only apparent literary influences are religious – Calle was of
too humble an origin to be affected by courtly literary fashions.

Chaucerian Comedy and Criseyde

Alfred David

1 Citations from Chaucer are to *The Works of Geoffrey Chaucer*, edited by
F. N. Robinson, 2nd edition (Boston, Massachusetts, 1957).

2   See D. W. Robertson, Jr., 'Chaucerian Tragedy', *English Literary History*, 19. (1952), 1–37, and Paul Strohm, '*Storie, Spelle, Geste, Romaunce, Tragedie*: Generic Distinctions in the Middle English Troy Narratives', *Speculum*, 46 (1971), 356–8.

3   John M. Steadman, *Disembodied Laughter; Troilus and the Apotheosis Tradition* (Berkeley, California, 1972). See especially pp. 88–93 on generic considerations.

4   See Robertson, *passim*; Ida L. Gordon, *The Double Sorrow of Troilus: A Study of Ambiguities in* Troilus and Criseyde (Oxford, 1970).

5   For a reading of the poem as the resolution of paradoxes (not necessarily ironies) in a *concordia discors*, see Donald W. Rowe, *O Love O Charite! Contraries Harmonized in Chaucer's* Troilus (Carbondale, Illinois, 1976).

6   As Lonnie Durham observes of these and other 'grave-bed' jokes: 'The metaphor implies all that Donne was later to make of it'. See 'Love and Death in *Troilus and Criseyde*', *Chaucer Review*, 3 (1968), 5.

7   Rowe (p. 80) makes the same point about her.

8   The mixture of comedy and tragedy in the poem has been often remarked. See, e.g., Helen Storm Corsa, *Chaucer: Poet of Mirth and Morality* (Notre Dame, Indiana, 1964), pp. 40–70; Willi Erzgräber, 'Tragic und Komic in Chaucer's "Troilus and Criseyde"', in *Festschrift für Walter Hübner* (Berlin, 1964), pp. 139–63; Steadman, pp. 88–93.

9   Albert C. Baugh, *Chaucer's Major Poetry* (New York, 1963), p. 558.

10 Medieval theory of comedy is based on an essay 'De tragoedia et comoedia', attributed to Donatus (actually two separate essays by different authors), containing a brief history of ancient drama. Comedy is defined rigidly and schematically in opposition to tragedy. See Madeleine Doran, *Endeavors of Art: A Study of Form in Elizabethan Drama* (Madison, Wisconsin, 1954), pp. 105–9, 415. There is no reason to suppose that Chaucer ever encountered this essay, which usually accompanied texts of Terence, but one statement from it bears on what I believe to be a crucial characteristic of Chaucerian comedy: 'tum quod in tragoedia fugienda uita, in comoedia capessenda exprimitur', rendered by Doran, 'then whereas in tragedy life is to be shunned, in comedy it is to be embraced'. See also Paul G. Ruggiers, 'Some Theoretical Considerations of Comedy in the Middle Ages', *Genre*, 9 (1976–77), 279–95.

11 See Paul G. Ruggiers, 'A Vocabulary for Chaucerian Comedy: A Preliminary Sketch', in *Medieval Studies in Honor of Lillian Herlands Hornstein* (New York, 1976), pp. 193–225, and Thomas J. Garbáty, 'Chaucer and Comedy', *Genre*, 9 (1976–77), 451–68.

12 Garbáty (pp. 451–2) suggests a theory of comedy is 'implied'.

13 Robertson, pp. 1–7.

14 Citations from *Il Filostrato* are from *Tutte le opere de Giovanni Boccaccio*, edited by Vittore Branca (Arnoldo Mondadori, 1964), Volume II.

15 C. S. Lewis, *The Allegory of Love* (Oxford, 1936), p. 185.

16 John M. Ganim, 'Tone and Time in Chaucer's *Troilus*', *English Literary*

History, 43 (1976), 142–3.

17 One critic who does wonder is E. T. Donaldson, 'Chaucer and the Elusion of Clarity', *Essays and Studies*, 25 (1972), 28–31. He includes an amusing 'inventory of Criseide's social situation'.

18 Note the use of anaphora in this speech, especially the thrice-repeated 'Allas!' (a fourth occurs in the omitted portion), a hallmark of Criseyde's tragic mode.

19 Lewis, p. 186.

20 Ibid., p. 185.

21 *The Book of Troilus and Criseyde*, edited by R. K. Root (Princeton, New Jersey, 1926), p. xxxii.

Troilus, Books I–III: A Criseydan reading

Mark Lambert

1 New York, 1969 (first published in London, 1936), p. 85.

2 The text quoted is *The Complete Works of Geoffrey Chaucer* edited by F. N. Robinson, 2nd edition (Boston, Massachusetts, 1957).

3 On Criseyde's much-explicated dream, see especially Joseph E. Gallagher, 'Criseyde's Dream of the Eagle: Love and War in *Troilus and Criseyde*', *MLQ* 36 (1975), 115–32.

4 When he first appears in the work, Troilus mocks the young knights love has made wretched. At the end, he laughs at the misery of those weeping for his death. Between the two scenes, he laughs not at all. The one quip that does at least make him smile is Pandarus's 'God have thi soule, ibrought have I thi beere' (II, 1638).

5 See also the discussion of Troy in Stephen A. Barney, 'Troilus Bound', *Speculum*, 47 (1972), 445–58 (pp. 457–8).

6 Even in the doctrinal passages on the power of love there is often something comfortable, and our awe before the might of Cupid is somewhat lessened by the narrator's slight complacency, his touch of smugness, when pointing to that might. Troilus, when compared to 'proude Bayard' pricked by his corn and lashed by his master, seems a less than august character, and the force that controls him not a very strange one.

7 'Ideals of Friendship', in *Patterns of Love and Courtesy: Essays in Memory of C. S. Lewis*, edited by John Lawlor (Evanston, Illinois, 1966), pp. 45–53 (p. 46). For a far more moral view of Chaucer's play with love and friendship than is presented in my essay, the reader should turn to Alan T. Gaylord, 'Friendship in Chaucer's *Troilus*', *Chaucer Review*, 3 (1968), 239–64.

8   Consider the only laps in Chaucer's beautifully constructed poem. In Deiphebus's house, it is 'by the lappe' that Pandarus brings Criseyde to Troilus (III, 59); later, in his own house, Pandarus guides Troilus 'by the lappe' to his niece (III, 742). Verbally, the heroine's sense of control in a frightening situation leads to her uncle's management of events.

9   Benoît de Sainte-Maure, *Roman de Troie*, 28429. Benoît's ringing denunciation of Helen is quoted by Singleton in his note to *Inferno*, V, 64 (Dante Alighieri, *The Divine Comedy, translated and with a commentary by Charles S. Singleton, Inferno* (2: Commentary) Princeton, New Jersey, 1970, pp. 79–80).

10   That in the Virgilian tradition Helen marries Deiphebus after the death of Paris is irrelevant here – or, better, relevant only as one more thing that makes the Chaucerian Helen a surprising figure, the scene at Deiphebus's house not what one might have expected. (For a discussion of the possibility that Chaucer wants us to think of Deiphebus and Helen as already lovers, see McKay Sundwall, 'Deiphebus and Helen: a Tantalizing Hint', *MP*, 73 (1975), 151–6. Sundwall's is a clear, sensible essay, but I find the interpretation he looks at unattractive as well as unnecessary.)

11   See H. M. Smyser, 'The Domestic Background of *Troilus and Criseyde*', *Speculum*, 31 (1956), 297–315.

12   See also Lewis, pp. 196–7: 'Outside is the torrential "smoky" rain which Chaucer does not allow us to forget; and who does not see what an innocent snugness, as of a children's hiding place, it draws over the whole scene?' Because Barney, in his exceptionally good article on the poem, connects images of containment in *Troilus* with the theme of bondage, it is perhaps important to emphasize containment need not be unpleasant. 'Troilus constantly finds himself in confined spaces: his bed . . ., the temple . . ., the closet . . ., the walls of Troy itself' (p. 457). Yes; but the audience of *Troilus* is at least subliminally aware that the innermost and least spacious chamber here is what the Wife of Bath calls the chamber of Venus. At Pandarus's house Troilus enters the closet, enters the bed, enters Criseyde: this is the underlying rhythm of the joyously comic central episode.

13   *Ricardian Poetry: Chaucer, Gower, Langland and the* Gawain *Poet* (London, 1971), pp. 126, 129.

Index